DEBORAH BRUCE

Deborah Bruce has been a theatre director for twenty years and has now started writing. Her other plays include *The Distance*, which was a finalist in the 2012–2013 Susan Smith Blackburn Prize, and *Same* for the National Theatre Connections Festival 2014.

Deborah Bruce

GODCHILD

NICK HERN BOOKS

London

www.nickhernbooks.co.uk

A Nick Hern Book

Godchild first published in Great Britain in 2013 as a paperback original by Nick Hern Books Limited, The Glasshouse, 49a Goldhawk Road, London W12 8QP

Godchild copyright © 2013 Deborah Bruce

Deborah Bruce has asserted her moral right to be identified as the author of this work

Cover image: iStockphoto/ElfriedeFleck
Cover design: Ned Hoste, 2H

Typeset by Nick Hern Books, London
Printed in Great Britain by Mimeo Ltd, Huntingdon, Cambridgeshire PE29 6XX

A CIP catalogue record for this book is available from the British Library

ISBN 978 1 84842 368 8

MIX
Paper from
responsible sources
FSC® C019549

Godchild was first performed at Hampstead Theatre Downstairs, London, on 31 October 2013. The cast was as follows:

MINNIE	Pearl Chanda
LOU	Tracy-Ann Oberman
KARL	Chook Sibtain
ANDY	Michael Shaeffer
Director	Michael Attenborough
Designer	Francesca Reidy
Lighting	Oliver Fenwick
Sound	John Leonard

For Jeremy

Characters

LOU, *forty*
MINNIE, *nineteen*
ANDY, *thirty-six*
KARL, *forty-two*

This text went to press before the end of rehearsals and so may differ slightly from the play as performed.

One

The kitchen in LOU*'s flat.*

LOU *is standing preparing gin and tonics.* MINNIE *is sitting at the kitchen table on the phone leaving a message.*

MINNIE. Hello, it's me, I've arrived safely, umm –

LOU (*shouting*). She's here, she's here!

MINNIE. Everything's fine, umm, yes, I'm here! So...

LOU (*shouting*). I'm plying her with gin! Hic! Chin chin!

MINNIE. Oh I left that washing, which is annoying, in the tumble dryer, but never mind, I'll get it at the weekend, or you could post it maybe, not the knickers, / just the blue top, maybe, if –

LOU. I've got knickers, you can have, do not worry, we have knickers, my darling child –

MINNIE. Well whatever, if you can be bothered to send it, / but it's fine.

LOU (*shouting, close to the phone, as she puts* MINNIE*'s gin on the table in front of her*). *Don't* worry, she is in very safe hands, hic! (*Laughing.*)

MINNIE (*suddenly very fast*). Anyway it's all fine call you in the morning hope you're okay love you bye! (*Hangs up.*)

LOU. Wahey! You're here!

MINNIE (*big exaggerated, whole-body relief*). I know! Oh my God!

LOU. My little Minnie Moo!

MINNIE *laughs.*

Minnie Moo with her blankie and her, what was it called, her, Doig Doig –

MINNIE (*laughing*). Mr Dog Dog –

LOU. Yes but you had to call it Doig Doig, 'Where's Mr Doig Doig?' Every time you came to stay we had to have Doig Doig, you could have gone without food for a week but you had to have that, what was it, a rabbit?

MINNIE. It was a dog –

LOU. You had to have Doig Doig, 'Where's Doig Doig?', every five bloody minutes. I remember it *so well*. So sweeeet! You're here my beautiful girl, cheers, *to you*. (*Calls out*.) Andy! We're doing cheers to Minnie! What the hell is he doing? We're doing the cheers and he's missing it! All the more gin for us. It's *so* exciting! Are you nervous? I remember my first day at university *so* well, I was shitting myself, are you shitting yourself? You *absolutely* don't need to be, honestly, Min, I am *absolutely* not bullshitting you –

ANDY *enters*.

Am I, Andy? It is *so* fun, honestly, all my memories of university are just loads and loads of *fun*.

MINNIE. I feel really nervous –

LOU. No. No, Minnie, stop that. Listen to me now. You have *nothing* to be nervous about. Everyone will love you as soon as they see you, of course they will. You are *so* gorgeous. Isn't she, Andy? And clever.

ANDY. Of course she's nervous –

LOU. Your drink's on the side. Yes but what I'm saying is there's no *reason* to be though. Because everyone is. And, everyone is so worried about how they are coming across that they won't have *time*, or *energy* to *judge* you or think anything about you at all in fact, thereby leaving you to be *absolutely* yourself. I mean it, Minnie, *now* is the time. You are liberated from the awful teenage years, *now*, it's *now*. Total liberation from that *hell*.

MINNIE. Aaah, thanks, Louise –

LOU. Believe me, lovely girl, you have arrived at the *best* bit, hasn't she, Andy?

ANDY. Who knows? Maybe.

LOU. I am so *jealous*! I am! Oh my God, when I think back to all the fun you are about to have! Minnie Moo!

MINNIE. Aaah, thank you. Cheers! And Andy as well. Thanks so much for letting me stay here.

LOU (*raising her hand, staccato*). Ach. *No*.

MINNIE. It's so kind of you –

LOU. Ach! Talk to the hand cos the face ain't listening.

Everything here is yours, there will be really big trouble if you don't treat this flat like your *absolute* home, I mean it, Minnie, there is *nothing* to thank me for. This is your *home*. We're flatmates! It's going to be so nice for *me*, I have been looking forward to it so much, having girly chats when I get in from work, and, and doing face packs and stuff. *Now*. I am not going to bother you with any of this now, *but*, we do have to schedule in a time to go through all the things you need to know, all the boring stuff – (*Does big bored action.*) bor-ing, I know, but we'll do it quickly, over a *gin*! More *gin*! Come on, get it down you!

MINNIE. Oh yes!

LOU (*gets up and prepares more gins*). You know, the back-door key, how that all works, the *bin*. The handle on the freezer door, that's jammed, you have to use this *spoon* to wrench it, it's fine, it's fine, I'm going to get it fixed anyway. Soon. You know, some other stuff, like the *shower* and the *heating*, it's on a timer thing, you have to slide it to the right if you want, oh I'll tell you when we're doing it, it's totally self-explanatory when you see it, all the *grown-up* boring bits, we'll go through it all another time when we can *bear* it. (*Opens and closes the freezer door with the spoon.*) You see, it's totally easy, can you see how I'm doing that?

MINNIE *looks, and nods*.

Hurray! One thing off the list! Don't worry about it, we'll set a time and go through it *all*. Very fast. So we don't lose the will to fucking *live*… (*A moment. She has said a bad thing. Recovers.*) When all me and you want to do is *chat* and drink *gin*! (*Hands her a gin.*) Don't we? Minnie Moo's all grown up now and we can be proper mates! To you! (*Clinks her glass.*)

MINNIE. To *you*.

LOU. To *you*, embarking on the *happiest* years of your life, oh my God, I can't wait for you to see how *great* it's going to be!

There is a small silence.

ANDY *opens and closes the freezer door.*

ANDY. There's nothing wrong with the door, it just needs defrosting.

LOU (*laughs and groans*). Ugh. Bor-ing. Whatever! There's nothing in it anyway, I only use it for ice! (*Nudges MINNIE.*) I'll tell you what, Andy, me and Min'll go to the pub, and you can stay here and defrost my freezer! (*Laughs.*)

MINNIE. Aaah, no, poor Andy.

LOU. Yeah? We'll see you later –

ANDY. I'm just saying –

LOU. We'll be in the pub, okay*?* (*Laughs.*)

ANDY. I couldn't care less about your freezer, I've got my own freezer to defrost thanks –

LOU. Right well good luck with that, we're off to the pub! (*Laughs.*)

ANDY. I'm just trying to say, you don't need the whole spoon, thing.

LOU. Thanks, Andy. That's very helpful. But I'm perfectly happy with my spoon arrangement, thanks. *Right!* Bedroom! Minnie. You are in the same bedroom you were always in, *however*, you may notice that since you last saw it it has come up in the world somewhat –

MINNIE. I know! I saw –

LOU. It is no longer a junk-stroke-dressing-stroke-full-of-any old-shit room, no, no. It is now rather 'bijou'. It is now rather 'des-res', it now actually has *curtains*, if you please, it now has *space*. In it.

MINNIE. I saw it when Andy put my bags. It's great!

LOU. It is now, An Adult Space.

MINNIE. It's lovely.

LOU. It's *your* space and I promise you I will not enter it unless invited. You can do *absolutely* whatever you wish to do in there. You can have friends over, private chats, sleepovers, you can have orgies! *Honestly!* You can do *whatever* you need to do. (*In a foreign accent.*) I ask no questions. Okay?

MINNIE. Thank you! I don't think I'll be having orgies but, you know...

LOU. You never know*!* (*Laughs.*)

MINNIE. Well, no.

ANDY. It's always nice to have the option.

ANDY and LOU exchange glances.

MINNIE. Well I'll bear it in mind.

Small silence.

LOU. Sweet angel.

ANDY and LOU stare at MINNIE.

I'm so *happy* you're *here*!

Small silence. ANDY moves to the window and looks out.

(*Cheerleader chant.*) Mi-nnee, Mi-nnee, Mi-nnee. Give us an M! Oh, Minnie's here!

MINNIE. Yay!

LOU. How *are* you?

MINNIE. I'm fine.

LOU. Sweetheart.

MINNIE. Honestly. I'm good.

LOU. Are you? Yeah?

MINNIE. It's lovely to be here with you.

LOU. Oh sweetheart, it's *so* lovely for me.

MINNIE (*laughs*). *Oh* I know what I was going to tell you, Louise –

LOU. *Anything*, you can tell me *absolutely* anything –

MINNIE. No it was just –

LOU. *Honestly*, Min, this is what I wanted to say to you, the only way this is going to work, is if we are *entirely* honest with each other and say *anything* that's bothering us *straight* away as soon as we think it, so *nothing* festers, nothing builds up into something, not that it would, but you can say *anything* you want to say to me, Min.

MINNIE. It's not a big deal it's just about this guy on the train.

LOU. Oh right?

MINNIE. He was like, looking over all the time and I was texting and stuff and he was like, looking over, he had headphones on but he kept looking over and I kept happening to be looking when he was looking and it was mad –

LOU. Oh *my God*! That's *hilarious*! He must have really fancied you, surprise surprise I wonder why –

MINNIE. No, it was weird cos I sort of thought I knew him from somewhere, but I wasn't sure, if you know what I mean –

LOU. Oh *yes*, it's *so* weird when that happens, I hate *that* –

MINNIE. Yeah, because you kind of think, oh they might be on television, or they might work in the shop –

ANDY. I saw Twiggy the other day –

LOU. No you didn't.

ANDY. I did. In Soho. Parking her car.

LOU. Bloody hell, Andy. Minnie doesn't know who Twiggy *is* for fuck's sake. She's from the bloody *olden* days! What. About. The *boy*?

MINNIE. No, just that we got chatting because the announcer bloke said something over the tannoy and it was So Funny because it sounded like, a foreign language, and everyone was like, What? And he was like, What the hell? And then he asked me where I was going and when I said, y'know, here, he said his friend, worked at Banner's, and I was like, oh my God, my godmother used to take me there for breakfast when I was little, and he was like, oh my God, how mad!

Slight pause.

LOU. Oh my God! How *funny*! What a tiny little world. What are the chances of that?

MINNIE. I know! I loved going to Banner's.

LOU. So did I! Let's go there every Sunday! Special Min and Lou time!

MINNIE. Okay!

Small silence. LOU *looks at* ANDY.

LOU. Andy, would you, can you nip to the shop for some wine? Minnie. Do you like red or white?

MINNIE. No, no, I meant to do that on the way, I'll go –

LOU. No, no, *absolutely not.* Andy'll go, Andy loves going to the shop, don't you?

ANDY (*laughs*). No!

LOU. Yes you do, you're always going to the shop! To get things.

ANDY. What are you talking about?

LOU. You!

MINNIE. I *want* to go, I want to get my bearings, I meant to do it on the way here, please let me.

MINNIE *is standing up and getting her bag.*

LOU. Well, I'm giving you the money –

LOU *gets her purse from the side.*

MINNIE. I've got money Mum gave me –

LOU. I am *not* having you spending your own money –

MINNIE. I'm going!

MINNIE *leaves the room.*

LOU (*calls after her*). I've got a fiver!

Sound of the front door opening as LOU *looks through her purse.*

MINNIE (*off*). See you in a minute!

Door slams.

LOU. Je-sus Christ. Oh fucking. *Fucking hell.*

ANDY *and* LOU *look at each other.*

What?

ANDY. Nothing.

LOU. Do you think she's alright? Do you? What do you think? Why aren't you *saying* anything?

ANDY. I'm exhausted.

LOU. *I'm* exhausted.

ANDY. It's you. You're exhausting. You're like a *Carry On* film.

LOU. Oh fuck off –

ANDY. You're insane.

LOU. I *know*. I don't know what the fuck I'm talking about. It's the *responsibility*. I'm overwhelmed. She's a nervous wreck –

ANDY. Well, we all are now. Just calm down –

LOU. I'm *trying* to be positive, I'm *being* supportive.

ANDY. It's freakish –

LOU. She's probably in tears round the corner –

ANDY. She'll be booking into a B & B if she's got any sense. Why can't you just be normal?

LOU. I'm being perfectly normal, I'm being *upbeat*. Jesus, at least I'm not being a *total* perv –

ANDY. What?

LOU. You said something *so* pervy about an orgy, *Je-sus* –

ANDY. What? You brought the whole orgy thing up, I was trying to bring it to a fucking close –

LOU. Well you sounded like a *total* paedophile –

ANDY. You started the orgy thing! 'Talk to the hand.' You're like Felicity Kendal at a youth club –

LOU. Well at least I'm *talking*, you're just *looming* –

ANDY. I'm mesmerised, you're like an American friend of someone's mother –

LOU. I think she's holding it all in. Do you?

ANDY. No.

LOU. Do you think she seems traumatised?

ANDY. She seems fine.

LOU. God, she's *so* different –

ANDY. She's probably just older, when did you last see her?

LOU. Don't be stupid, shut up.

ANDY. Well I've never met her so that's three years at least –

LOU. Oh *God*, what's wrong with me, why can't I *do* this?

ANDY. Just be you –

LOU. I *am* me, this *is* me, you idiot. Shall I send her a text?

ANDY. Yes. Because that's a really normal thing to do isn't it.

LOU. I'm hysterical! I need a – (*Hysterically mimes smoking a cigarette*.)

ANDY. What?

LOU. I need a – (*Mimes inhaling*.)

ANDY. A cigarette?

LOU. Shhh.

ANDY. Why?

LOU (*hissed*). *Minnie!*

ANDY. She's at the shop.

LOU. Jesus Christ.

ANDY. For God's sake, just have a cigarette. (*Pause*.) How long's she staying?

LOU. I don't know, until she gets some confidence, until she's secure in her environment, Mel said.

ANDY. You're going to have to chill the fuck out.

LOU scrabbles about in her bag and gets a cigarette. She goes to the back door. She has to do something quite complicated to open it involving her knee and lifting the door up. She can't do it.

LOU. *Je-sus*, it's *you*. You're making me feel like I've fucked it all up now.

ANDY opens the back door for her. LOU lights the cigarette and holds it as far away from the kitchen as she can, wafting the smoke away.

And I have to warn her about upstairs.

ANDY. Don't get her involved in all that –

LOU. How can I not? She's not blind and deaf.

ANDY. Don't make a drama out of it –

LOU. I'm not, I'm just saying, it's totally doing my head in.

ANDY. Yeah. Well. Minnie doesn't need to get into all that.

LOU. The sooner they take that baby off her the better.

ANDY. Don't mention all that tonight.

LOU. Minnie's bound to bump into her.

ANDY. Just don't get involved.

LOU. What do you mean, 'don't get involved'? Like what? Stay in?

ANDY. Move in with me.

LOU. Oh Andy, please.

Pause. They have had this conversation loads of times.

I can't get into this now, I'm too stressed out.

ANDY. I don't understand what we're waiting for.

LOU. Andy! I can't talk about this now. I'm too *stressed* to even *think* about talking about it now –

ANDY. I'm just saying, we're obviously going to do it one day, I don't understand what we're waiting for –

LOU. Well Minnie's staying now, so.

LOU*'s phone beeps*. LOU *reads a text*.

ANDY. Anyway. Just don't make a big thing of upstairs to Minnie.

Pause.

LOU. She's been ages, do you think something's happened to her?

ANDY. No.

LOU. I'm *supposed* to be keeping her safe. I'm *supposed* to be providing a *secure* environment.

ANDY. She's in a shop –

LOU. I'm *supposed* to be the responsible fucking adult –

ANDY. She's not a baby.

LOU (*scoffs*). *Supposed* to be fucking parentis locis, whatever the fuck –

ANDY. *In loco parentis*. She's nineteen.

LOU. Going loco in fucking *Acapulco* more like. (*Stubs out her cigarette and comes in, wafting smoke away*.) I'm going to fuck this up, I know I am. I'm not responsible enough for this… *responsibility*.

ANDY. She's responsible for herself, you keep saying to her, she's all grown up and stuff –

LOU. I *said* that, yes, I *said* that. I'm *empowering* her, I'm trying to make her feel *confident*. You have *absolutely* no idea what she's been through, she's fragile, she's not like a London teenager, she's emotionally… Mel said she was *this* close to turning down the place. We have to bolster her up. Well, *you* don't, it's my *responsibility*, as a designated responsible person, in her life.

ANDY. God help her.

LOU. Yes. Quite.

Silence.

God! I need some drugs or something. I really need something to chill me out.

ANDY. She's only been here twenty minutes –

LOU. I know! I can't do it can I?

ANDY. Of course you can.

LOU. I'll have to score some drugs –

ANDY. Nip upstairs, they should be able to sort you out –

LOU. Do you think Minnie'll have anything? You keep a lookout, I'll search her bags.

ANDY. Are you serious?

LOU. No, of course I'm not, she's my *god*-daughter.

LOU *comes in and shuts the back door.* ANDY *leaves the room.* LOU *wipes a surface and refills the ice tray. She opens the freezer with the spoon and puts the ice back.* ANDY *enters with his coat on.*

Where are you *going*?

ANDY. Home. Well, I might meet Guy for a drink at The Crown, I texted him.

LOU. You can't *leave* me with her.

ANDY. What? Why not?

LOU. You can't *leave* me.

ANDY. Okay, I can come back later if you want.

LOU. No no no.

The door buzzer goes.

Oh fucking *great*, who's that?

ANDY. It'll be Minnie won't it?

LOU. Oh yes. *Please*, Andy, *please* you can't leave me, I can't *do* it, I'm having a panic attack in my chest, what if she breaks down? What if she starts to freak out? Text Guy, tell him to come here, why can't you meet him tomorrow? *Please*, Andy.

MINNIE *comes into the flat.*

MINNIE (*calls*). Hello!

LOU (*calls*). Hi!

MINNIE *enters kitchen with two bottles of wine.*

MINNIE. That was embarrassing –

LOU. How did you get in?

MINNIE. Upstairs buzzed me in, I didn't know which buzzer to press so I pressed both. I bought one red and one white I didn't remember what you wanted.

LOU. Well, I'm *definitely* going to give you the money.

MINNIE. I was like, 'Is that Louise?' She was like, 'No,' I was like, 'Oh sorry, can you let me in?' She was like, bzzzzzz. It was *so* embarrassing.

LOU. And then how did you get in my door, did you leave it on the latch?

MINNIE. Yeah, I just left it open, so I –

LOU. Yeah, don't do that.

MINNIE. Oh. Right. Sorry.

LOU. No, it's just. Don't, y' know, it's better if you don't, because… *Oh my God*, I *have* to give you a *key. Sweetheart!* I'm so *sorry*. I had you a key cut, of course I did, I'm such an idiot, why are we even *having* this, this this, *situation*? I've got you a key!

LOU *rushes out the room.*

MINNIE *and* ANDY *stand in the kitchen.* MINNIE *looks at* ANDY. ANDY *smiles at* MINNIE.

ANDY. She's got you a key cut.

MINNIE. Great.

Pause.

I got red and white, so…

ANDY. Nice one.

LOU (*off*). I put it somewhere clever! It's totally fucking. Disappeared! I can't remember what coat I was wearing!

ANDY *and* MINNIE *stand there.*

ANDY. She's got loads of coats.

ANDY *and* MINNIE *stand in silence.*

So where do you live again?

MINNIE. Woodbridge.

ANDY. Oh yeah, Sussex.

MINNIE. Suffolk.

ANDY. Suffolk, cool.

Pause.

So, London, hey?

LOU *enters.*

LOU. I can't find it. Andy, give her your key.

ANDY. Oh, really?

LOU. Well you don't need it do you?

ANDY. Don't I? Have we split up?

LOU. Don't be stupid, you don't need it *now*, do you?

MINNIE. It's okay, I can wait for you to find it.

LOU (*to* ANDY). I'll get you another one, give her yours.

ANDY *takes a while to take the key off the keyring.*

Sorry about that, Min, it's probably *fine* to leave the door ajar if you're just popping to the bin or something but, you know, it's not like, you probably shouldn't, the woman in the upstairs flat is a bit. She's *sweet*, but just a bit. Disorganised. About boundaries. Sometimes. You know. *Anyway*, enough bollocks, let's get this wine open. Andy, what are you doing then? Standing there.

ANDY. Well –

LOU. Are you meeting Guy?

ANDY. Well, not if –

LOU. Go go go, Minnie and I don't want a *boy* hanging around for God's sake, do we, Min? No boys allowed! Girls-only zone, thank you!

ANDY. Oh right, okay. Are you sure?

LOU. Of course I'm sure!

    ANDY *stands about in his coat for a bit.* MINNIE *sits down and checks her phone.* LOU *struggles with the bottle opener.*

ANDY. Do you want me to do that?

    LOU *hands him the bottle.*

LOU. Put some music on, Min, choose something. Choose whatever you like. We're going to have a brilliant night, the first of many more, my lovely *flatmate*!

    MINNIE *takes up* LOU*'s iPod and scrolls through.*

MINNIE. You've got some brilliant old stuff, this is so cool.

    ANDY *hands* LOU *the open bottle of wine.* MINNIE *places the iPod in the speaker. The chosen track is 'We Are Your Friends' by Justice vs Simian.* LOU *dances.*

ANDY (*loudly over the high volume of the music*). Okay, so you're okay if I go then, is that right?

LOU. You said you were meeting Guy, aren't you meeting him?

ANDY. Yeah, you're okay with that?

LOU. Yes. (*Laughs.*) Thank you, I think we'll manage.

ANDY. Okay. Bye then, Minnie, nice to meet you –

MINNIE. Nice to meet you, Andy, yes –

ANDY. Good luck for tomorrow.

LOU. She won't need good luck, look at her.

ANDY. Okay well have a good time anyway.

MINNIE. Thanks!

ANDY. And I'm sure I'll see you again.

LOU. Of course you'll see her again – (*Laughing.*) 'I'm sure I'll
see you again.' She *lives* here now, she's my new best friend,
my NBF.

MINNIE. See you, Andy. See you soon.

LOU. What time do you have to be there tomorrow, Min?

MINNIE. I don't know it says in the pack thing.

LOU. What are you going to wear?

MINNIE. I don't know!

LOU. Get the pack, get the pack!

    ANDY *kisses* LOU *goodbye*.

    Call me later.

ANDY. Okay.

LOU. Call me from the pub.

ANDY. Okay.

LOU. Text me or something.

ANDY. Okay.

LOU. Whatever.

ANDY. Will do.

    ANDY *stands there for a moment*.

    So, I haven't got a key now remember. So…

LOU. I know, that's fine. We'll let you in if you come to the
door on a dark and stormy night, won't we, Minnie? We'll
let you in.

MINNIE. We will.

ANDY. Okay good. (*Pause*.) Bye then.

MINNIE *and* LOU. Bye!

ANDY *stands a moment. And then leaves. The front door closes behind him.*

MINNIE. Aaaah, he's really sweet.

LOU. I know.

LOU *brings two glasses of wine to the table and sits.*

Too fucking sweet. Je-sus, Minnie, he's doing my head in. I just don't know how to finish it. Fuck me, it is *so* over, this relationship has *absolutely* outstayed its welcome.

LOU *picks up her phone and starts to send a text while she's talking.*

You *have* to help me, I'm *suffocating*, I mean it, I feel totally *strangulated* by him. Honestly, Min, the *sole* purpose of your staying here has to be to *sort out my life*. You're so sensible, Min, you've always been sensible, you were sensible when you were two. A wise old owl. Me and Mel would sit at the kitchen table in Sandford Street talking for *hours* about, whatever, you know, our *problems*, boys, probably. And you would come over and put your little hand on my hand and look up, with such, *understanding*, honestly, I'm not making it up, Minnie, you *knew* about stuff, you stopped me in my tracks, you were saying, you know, it's okay.

MINNIE. Oh, but Andy's really sweet, Louise.

LOU. I know! That's why it's so *awful* for me, I'm in *total* turmoil about it.

LOU*'s phone rings, she jumps and squeals, then answers.*

Did you get my text?... You're joking, I just sent you a text... Just *now*, like ten seconds ago... Oh my God, how *weird* is that?... Well, here I am...

LOU *walks out of the kitchen, she is coy and laughing and saying 'yeah', 'yeah'. MINNIE sits still, listening, and looking around the room. After a while she gets her keys out of her pocket and attaches them to her other keys on a key ring.*

LOU *hovers in the doorway mouthing 'Sorry', rolling her eyes and miming pouring a glass of wine.*

MINNIE *goes to pour the wine and knocks the wine glass with her arm.*

The glass smashes.

Blackout.

Two

LOU *is having a phone conversation in the blackout. Gradually, over her speaking, she is revealed to be sitting on a window ledge outside a room in* KARL's *flat. The flat is in total darkness. Sound of occasional cars passing from the street below.*

LOU. I'm at the bus stop… Waiting for a bus obviously. I'm so tired, I just want to *crawl* into bed as soon as I get in the door. Everyone at work today was saying, 'God, you look *so* tired.' I don't know what's wrong with me. I feel *whacked*, I feel *drained*, I feel *squeezed* out… Yeah, I will… Yeah, I'm going to… Yeah, I will… Thank you, darling… Yeah, I will, I know… Aaaaah. That's so sweet… Aaaaah, yeah. I will… Okay! Here's my bus! Thank God! Okay!… Okay… Yeah, and you, yeah, and you… I will… I promise, big kiss, big kiss, bye, bye.

LOU *ends the call. A car has been pulling up outside over the end of her conversation. The car door opens and slams.* LOU *calls down.*

Did you find somewhere? Did you get it? Did you have to go to the garage?

The sound from inside the flat of a key in the door, opening, closing.

Couldn't you find anywhere open?

LOU *stares uncertainly into the darkness.*

What are you doing? (*Pause.*) Karl?

The electricity comes back on. All the lights. Machines whirr into action, music comes on the stereo. LOU *leans into the room to an ashtray and takes out half a spliff and relights it. After a while* KARL *enters carrying a pasty on a plate.*

Well done.

KARL. Thank you very much.

LOU. You were ages.

KARL. Did you miss me?

LOU. I did actually.

KARL. I'll pay you back, remind me. Do you want half this pasty?

LOU. I'll have a bite.

LOU *swaps the spliff for the pasty.* KARL *climbs out and sits next to* LOU *on the windowsill. They are very physical with each other.*

So are you going to tell me the truth or have you spent –

KARL *(laughing)*. I can't believe you are still thinking about –

LOU *(laughing)*. – the last half an hour coming up with a story…

KARL. I don't care if you don't believe me…

LOU. If you haven't got a kid why would you have a child seat in your car? Why would a childless person… I don't care if you've got kids, why won't you just admit / it?

KARL. I haven't got fucking kids. Why would I lie about it? *(Laughing.)* Man. This is so stupid, why would I say I didn't have a kid if I had a kid. / Why would I say that?

LOU. I don't know. So why have you got a child seat in your car?

KARL *(laughing)*. What?

LOU. You haven't given me a good, you don't have a proper explanation…

KARL. Are you arresting me?

LOU. Why would someone…

KARL. Can I phone my solicitor?

LOU (*laughing*). Shut up. Why can't I ask you? Is it weird that I want to know?

KARL. There's nothing to know. I told you why it's there, there's nothing sinister, I told you…

LOU. What, what did you tell me? I don't care if you've got kids…

KARL. Thanks, that's very gracious. Right, I haven't got kids. (*Pause*.) I've just got a kid's seat.

LOU. Where's it come from?

KARL (*laughing*). I don't know. It's always been there. You just didn't notice it.

LOU. I would have noticed it. (*Pause*.) It's odd.

KARL. I'm odd.

LOU. Forget it. You don't have to tell me. Obviously.

KARL (*laughing*). Okay.

    Pause. KARL *makes a move on* LOU.

LOU. And you're such a *liar*! The crap about the police not pulling you over if you have one?

KARL. It's true!

LOU. Why would the police pull you over? What are you going to be doing that's suspicious? You mean speeding?

KARL. They don't need a reason.

LOU. If you're speeding how can they see the car seat? You are such a *liar*. (*Laughing*.) It's fine, don't tell me.

    Pause.

KARL (*laughing*). I don't have a kid.

LOU. It's fine. You don't have to tell me anything.

KARL (*laughing*). I'd tell you if I did.

LOU. It's cool. Talk about something else.

    Pause.

KARL. Are you still with your bloke?

LOU. Yeah. Kind of.

KARL. Oh good.

> KARL *gets a lighter out of his pocket and starts to build a spliff.*

LOU. Yeah, that's more like it, get the drugs out.

> *Short silence.*

KARL. So. Where've you been?

LOU. I don't know.

KARL. Where've you been all my life?

LOU. Nowhere.

KARL. Not here though.

LOU. No.

KARL. Or answering your phone.

> LOU *shakes her head.*

LOU. I don't know what to say to you. I feel bad.

KARL. Don't feel bad. It's cool. Don't worry about it.

> *Short silence.*

LOU. Let's do something. What do you want to do?

KARL. What do *you* want to do?

LOU. Go for a late drink. Let's get fucked off our faces. Drive me to a hostelry!

KARL. Okay. I'm skint. And I've got no petrol.

LOU. I've got money.

KARL. Let's go. (*Pause.*)

> I've missed you. Not because of your money.

LOU. Yeah, right. (*Pause.*)

> I wanted to phone you.

KARL. It's cool.

LOU. It's been weird.

Silence for a bit. LOU *finishes the spliff,* KARL *concentrates on the one he is building.*

I've had someone staying, just the daughter of a friend, well my sort of god-daughter really, only she didn't have a christening, y'know, so it's not officially. She's a bit, fucked up.

KARL. What, cos she didn't have a christening?

LOU. God, how's your *dad*?

KARL. Not great. He's a bit, fucked up too.

LOU. Oh. Sorry. Have you been to see him today?

KARL. No. I was going to. But I had to wait in for Mack, and that was like two hours. My sister went up there, my half-sister was going up tonight. He's asleep most of the time anyway.

Pause.

I fucking hate that hospital.

LOU. Are you going to go tomorrow then?

KARL. Yeah. If I can. Why? Do y'wanna come?

LOU. No!

KARL. Here you are, babe, do you want this?

KARL *passes her the spliff. She takes it.*

LOU. So is he drugged up to the eyeballs then?

KARL. He has to take, like, fourteen pills a day. He has to take a pill to settle his stomach because he's taking so many pills. He's got this rash, his hands are shaking all the time. The anti-rejection drugs just fuck with your immune system. Apart from that, he's great. He's thinking of training for the marathon. So, you know. Hey-ho, it's not all bad.

KARL*'s mobile phone rings.*

That'll be him now. From the gym.

KARL *looks at the caller ID and rejects the call.* LOU *checks her phone.*

What's with the kid?

LOU. She's not really a kid, she's nineteen. She's stressed. She's had a difficult time.

KARL. She needs to chill out.

LOU. Is that your, diagnosis?

KARL. Yeah. I prescribe a course of recreational medication.

LOU. Doctor, what the *fuck* is your last name?

KARL. A-ha!

LOU. Seriously, fucking hell, what is your second name?

KARL. Mmmm, now, let's see.

LOU. I can't believe I don't know that, do I know it? Have I known your name? Just tell me, I *do* know, don't I? What the fuck is it?

KARL *stares at her blankly.*

What is it? (*Laughing.*) Stop it! Karl. You're freaking me out. What is it? What's your name?

KARL *remains totally blank.*

I'm having a panic attack, stop it! I'm going to cry! Don't make me go in and find your post.

KARL *laughs.*

Tell me!

KARL. *That* is a threat.

LOU. Shut up, tell me your fucking name.

KARL. I like your style, girl, that is one hell of a threat, you could be a gangsta –

LOU. Tell me it –

KARL. Seriously, Lou, I'm sweating here. Break my fingers, fuck my sister, but don't go in and find my post. I'm shitting myself.

LOU. *Fine*. Don't tell me.

KARL. Reverse psychology, cool.

LOU. You're irritating me now.

KARL. Threaten to find my post again.

LOU. No. Make another spliff.

KARL. Threaten to find my post and I'll tell you my name.

LOU. No, I don't even care what your name is now, I want more spliff.

KARL (*laughing*). Did you have a hard day?

LOU. Fuck off.

KARL. Did you though?

LOU. I mean it, Karl, I'm feeling fragile now.

KARL. Oh, babe, I'm only mucking about, it's good, it's great what you do. Whatever it is.

LOU. Fuck off. At least my job exists.

KARL. It's great that it does. I'm serious. It's great you exist. Come here.

A moment where they both consider sex. Then the sound of a car pulling up downstairs, very loud bass and three blasts on the horn.

(*Shouts down.*) Oi! (*To* LOU.) Hang on. (*Climbs into the flat.*) I'll be back in a minute.

LOU. Who is it?

KARL. Mack. I'll be back in a sec. (*Exits.*)

LOU watches them on the street. Sound of their conversation, laughter, over the car stereo. KARL is saying he has to go to Peckham. LOU climbs into the room. She checks her phone and gathers her things. KARL returns. He has a whole load of money in his hand. He takes a couple of notes and puts them in his back pocket. He gives a tenner to LOU, and puts the rest in a drawer.

Thanks. For the leccy key.

LOU *takes the money*.

LOU. I'm going to go.

KARL. What?

LOU. I just, I don't know. I shouldn't be here really.

KARL. Yes you should. Come on. I've got cash now. We can go out.

LOU. How come you've got so much money?

KARL. I'm incredibly rich.

LOU. Okay. (*Pause*.) I just think I should go.

KARL. Okay.

KARL *starts to roll a joint. He sits on the sofa. No one says anything for a while*.

What's going on?

LOU. I hate this. I can't do this. I don't know. It's all so messy.

KARL. Mess is good, man. Sit.

LOU. I should get back for Minnie.

KARL. Who?

LOU. My friend's daughter, she's *staying* –

KARL. The godchild.

LOU. I'm *supposed* to be looking after her.

KARL. I thought you said she was nineteen.

LOU. Yeah, but. She's only been here a couple of weeks. I haven't left her on her own yet, I didn't say I wouldn't be home. She's not good at night. She'll wonder where I am.

KARL. Text her and tell her where you are.

LOU. I've got a missed call from her already.

KARL. Call her then.

LOU. She'll think it's weird.

KARL. What's weird about it?

LOU. She'll wonder who you are if I say I'm staying here.

KARL. Say something else then.

LOU. You know, what the fuck am I doing here? I mean, what the *fuck* am I doing? Basically. (*Pause*.) I'm tired. All this shit. With the idiots upstairs. Her boyfriend's back, slamming doors at three in the morning. Shouting.

Silence.

KARL. Just move…

LOU. Yeah. (*Pause*.) It's crazy. (*Pause*.) Sorry. You've got proper stuff going on with your dad.

KARL. My dad and his dead man's heart. Crash here if you want.

LOU (*laughs*). Jesus *Christ*, I can't *crash* somewhere, I'm not sixteen.

KARL. So?

LOU. I can't *crash*. Teenagers *crash*, I'm *supposed* to be. It's bad enough that I'm still renting, I can't stop renting and *crash*. I'm supposed to be a *grown-up*!

KARL. Crash like a grown-up then, I don't care, I'm just saying, you can stay here if you're freaked out by the junkies.

KARL *clambers onto* LOU *on the sofa*. KARL *touches* LOU*'s face very tenderly*.

Don't go away again.

LOU *doesn't say anything*.

Okay, you can. But make sure you come back.

LOU. Yeah. Okay.

Pause. LOU *looks away*.

You are so shady.

KARL. Yeah, yeah, you love it.

KARL*'s phone rings. He checks caller ID and rejects the call*.

Let's go out.

LOU. Do you want to, yeah?

KARL. Do you?

KARL's landline rings. He doesn't move to answer it.

LOU. Is everything alright?

KARL. It's my mum.

LOU. Shouldn't you answer it?

KARL. It's okay.

LOU. Do you want to go over there?

KARL. No, of course I don't. I want to be here, with you.

KARL's mobile goes, he looks at the caller ID and answers straight away.

(*On phone.*) Hey… Just walking out the door, mate, why?

KARL leaves the room. LOU *stands up.* KARL *comes back in the room still on the phone.*

Yeah, yeah, just be quick, mate. Beep the horn, I'll run down. Okay.

(*Hangs up.*) We have to wait two minutes. My mate's round the corner, he has to drop something off. Do you want something? Do you want a cup of black tea?

LOU. No, I'm okay.

LOU sits down again.

KARL. Can't get out the fucking house at the moment.

He sits down next to her on the sofa. He kisses her. He undoes her top.

I love the smell of you. I can smell you for days on my sheets.

LOU. Are you sure it's me?

KARL. Oh yes, it's you.

LOU. What, you can just about make me out?

KARL. Yeah, just about.

They are kissing. A car horn beeps loudly outside. KARL
sits up.

LOU. That was quick.

KARL. No messing. (*Gets up and goes out.*) I won't be a
minute.

Voices downstairs, LOU *goes to the window and looks out.
She steps back suddenly.*

KARL *returns. He has a whole load of money in his hand.
He takes a couple of notes and puts them in his back pocket.
He gives a tenner to* LOU, *and puts the rest in a drawer.*

Thanks. For the leccy key.

LOU. You gave me it.

KARL. What?

LOU. You gave me ten quid, a minute ago.

KARL. For real? Fuck. My head.

I've got cash now. We can go out.

Pause.

LOU. How come you've got so much money?

KARL. I'm a multimillionaire.

LOU. Okay.

I think I should go.

KARL *starts to roll a joint. He sits on the sofa. No one says
anything for a while.*

LOU *doesn't go.*

It's just Minnie. I'm too distracted. Worrying about her.

KARL. Who?

LOU. Minnie, my godchild.

KARL. Yeah, man.

Pause.

LOU. And. I should be in work for half-eight. I was late today.

KARL *gives* LOU *a look*.

What?

KARL. Keep it simple, keep it simple, girl.

LOU. What?

KARL. Don't start lying to *me*.

KARL *looks at her with a face*.

LOU. Don't be horrible about him.

KARL. What did I say?

LOU. He's actually a really sweet man.

KARL. Whoa! Fucking hell! I hope you never say that about me.

LOU. I don't.

KARL. You are fucked up. (*Laughs*.) You are one fucking, fucked-up fuck.

Pause.

What's so great about him then? Come on, let's have it.

LOU. I don't want you to ask me that.

KARL. No? Let's do this.

LOU. I'm not going to.

KARL. Y'know, you should write a list of all the things I'm not allowed to ask you.

LOU. You can talk!

KARL. Topics of conversation that are strictly off-limits.

LOU. What about your list!

LOU *picks up a pen and something to write on*. KARL *is smoking the joint*.

Oh my God! Bring it on!

KARL *takes the pen off* LOU.

KARL. What's his name?

LOU (*laughing*). Okay, don't make me tell you that –

KARL (*writing it down*). What's. His. Name?

LOU. Give me the pen –

> *They are laughing, fighting over the pen,* KARL *is easily winning.*

> Okay why have you got a child's car seat, and, *apparently*, no child?

KARL. You *can* ask me that –

LOU. Write it down!

KARL. No. I let you ask me that question, I answered that question, therefore, that question does not belong on this list –

> (*Writing.*) Where have you been for the last three weeks?

LOU. What the fuck is your job?

KARL (*a look like she's talking nonsense*). You know what my job is –

LOU. But you can't tell me, write it down! / You are such a cheat.

KARL (*looks at* LOU). You know what I do. Don't pretend you don't. (*Writes.*) Why won't you let me come to your flat?

LOU. Okay. Well, that's obvious. Okay, okay, whose were those earrings in your bathroom that time? Yes? Thank you. Write that down –

KARL (*stops writing and looks at her*). They were Jade's. Why can't I come to your flat?

LOU. Hang on, who the fuck is Jade? That *girl*? That *child*? (*Laughing*) That fifteen-year-old in the car that time? Write this down, you are refusing to answer –

KARL. You have no right to ask me, that's different –

LOU. Write Jade down, you're a fucking cheat –

KARL. I'll tell you if you want me to, so, it doesn't belong on the list –

LOU. Alright, give me the pen, here we go, your dad – write him down – Why You Never Seem to be able to get it Together to Go and Visit your dad in Hospital even though he is Seriously ill and could Drop Dead any minute.

They stare at each other, a bit shocked, KARL *laughs, then* LOU *does.*

KARL. Okay. Hell. What happened there?

LOU. Sorry, but y'know. You can talk.

Silence.

KARL. Fucking hell. How did that get so dark?

LOU. I can't even read most of this.

LOU *is looking at the list.*

What does that even say?

KARL. What's his name?

LOU. Andy.

Pause... KARL *gets up.*

KARL. Okay. You're right. I don't need to know this stuff. That doesn't feel good.

If I made a risotto would you eat some?

He goes into the kitchen.

LOU. What time is it? What are you going to put in it?

KARL (*calling*). Leeks? Hang on. No leeks. Onion.

LOU. An onion risotto.

KARL (*coming back in*). I've got some brie.

LOU. That doesn't sound right.

Pause.

I need to sleep.

Pause.

Aren't you tired?

KARL. I didn't get up till four.

LOU. Was it getting dark?

KARL. A bit. The day was on its way out.

Pause.

LOU. I hate that.

Pause.

I'm going to go home now.

LOU *stays seated.*

KARL *goes over to* LOU *and holds out his hand to pull her up.*

What are we doing?

KARL. Going to bed.

LOU *doesn't stand up.*

Come on. We've run out of things we're allowed to talk about.

LOU *looks.*

(*Laughing.*) I'm only mucking about, come on.

LOU *is silent.*

Okay. Go home then.

LOU *stands up.*

This night's beginning to get on my nerves anyway.

LOU. Sorry for what I said about your dad.

KARL. Come here.

They hug.

You do get to know whose heart you've got by the way. I asked my mum. You can know all that stuff if you want.

LOU. Really? Who –

KARL. Just some bloke. Forty-four. My dad knows his name.

LOU. Really?

Pause.

KARL. Some people make contact with the family of the donor and get all matey and stuff. My sister was saying that this one guy got flowers every year from the donor's wife on their wedding anniversary. How morbid is that?

LOU *bursts into tears*.

What's happened?

LOU. That's so sad.

KARL (*laughing*). Don't cry about it.

LOU. Doesn't that make you feel a bit sad?

KARL. It makes me feel a bit sick.

LOU. I don't know what's wrong with me, that really is the saddest thing.

KARL (*goes to her, laughing*). Come here, what are you crying for? He's *my* dad.

LOU. I know! I don't know what's wrong with me. God, I'm so sorry I said he was going to die, on the list. I'm all over the place. I feel so adrift.

KARL. It's the weed. That weed is strong shit.

LOU. No, it's before. It's before now. It's me, I'm not sleeping, and I can't even get up in the night because I don't want to wake Minnie. In case she starts *talking* to me, I just want to be on my own. She's doing my head in, if I'm honest about it. She's just *there*. I'm so *old*. I feel like I'm nineteen, but I can't be because she is. That's what nineteen looks like, there she is. It *feels* recent. It feels like no distance between here and there. But there is. When did that happen? Is there a day when it happens, or do you look back and just see that it has? It's like, all I can feel is the *gap* between then and now, but I haven't landed anywhere, I don't feel *now*. My life is just hanging in this *gap*. I'm suspended there.

KARL *hands her the spliff*. LOU *takes it*.

Yeah. Cos that'll help.

I thought it would be nice having her around. But. She puts sell-by dates in her diary, she's so, odd.

KARL. She puts what?

LOU. She's got a weird thing with food. She writes the sell-by dates in her diary, yogurts and stuff. I don't know.

KARL's mobile phone rings. He looks at caller ID and switches it off.

Who was that?

KARL looks at her for a moment and shrugs.

So what am I leaving my boyfriend for?

KARL. You're not leaving your boyfriend.

LOU. Oh yeah.

Pause.

KARL. It's cool.

LOU. Yeah. (*Pause.*) It's not cool.

KARL (*goes over to his iPod, scrolls for a song and puts it in the speaker dock*). Hey! Listen to this song.

The song plays. It is soulful. They sit and listen for a while and then KARL gently pulls LOU up to dance with him. They are very close and calm.

Lights fade.

Three

LOU*'s front room/kitchen. It is night.* MINNIE *is in her pyjamas standing by the open back door. There is torchlight moving around in the garden.*

MINNIE. I'm sorry, Andy.

ANDY (*off*). There's no footprints in this muddy bit.

MINNIE. I'm obviously just imagining things –

ANDY (*off*). There's no evidence of anyone climbing over the wall –

MINNIE. I'm probably going mad!

ANDY. Which is the only access point into these gardens –

MINNIE. I'm really sorry but I didn't know who else to call.

ANDY (*off*). Really, it's fine, I was just about to get on the Tube anyway…

　　ANDY *appears in the doorway.*

MINNIE. It really did sound like a person. Skulking about. I feel like an idiot, I've totally wasted your time.

ANDY (*coming in and wiping his feet*). No you haven't, it's just as easy for me to come here as it is to go home.

MINNIE. I was trying to get hold of Louise you see –

ANDY. Better to be safe than, y'know, bludgeoned to death in the kitchen! –

MINNIE. I thought Louise might have been with you, when I couldn't get through to her on her phone.

　　ANDY *closes and locks the back door.*

ANDY. It's fine. There's no one out there. It'll have been a fox.

MINNIE. I didn't want to call the police, because I thought that might have been a bit. Over-the-top.

ANDY. Oh God yes, totally.

MINNIE. I feel embarrassed now, for calling you, I panicked.

ANDY (*laughing*). You know, if it had been a fox with a flick knife, wearing a balaclava, now that would have been different.

MINNIE. Well anyway, if you want to go home now, I'm sure I'll be fine.

ANDY. Don't be silly, I'm here now, I'll wait for Lou. She'll be home in a minute anyway.

ANDY moves into the sitting room. He takes off his coat. MINNIE follows him.

MINNIE. Well she might not be.

ANDY. She'll be home any minute, it's the last Tube about now.

MINNIE. I did call her but her phone must be off. Or something.

ANDY. I spoke to her earlier. She's at a work thing, someone's leaving, they've gone for a meal, she was tired, it won't be a late one.

MINNIE. Oh okay.

MINNIE stands about, she looks fearful. She turns on some lamps and looks out the window.

ANDY. Don't let me stop you. Getting on with your. Whatever you'd be doing if.

MINNIE. Okay.

Small silence. MINNIE stays standing there.

ANDY. So! How's university?

MINNIE. Yeah!

ANDY. Are you having a great time, yeah? Meeting loads of people? God, university's brilliant isn't it?

MINNIE. Yeah, it's great.

ANDY. Excellent news.

ANDY goes out into the hall. MINNIE makes a sudden, panicked movement while he is gone. He returns with a backpack.

ANDY *sits down and takes out a pile of papers.*

If you don't mind. I'm going to do this marking.

MINNIE. Oh right. No, not at all, of course!

ANDY. Might as well.

MINNIE *watches him for a while.*

Jesus Christ, the shit these kids come up with.

There is the sound of some doors slamming upstairs, and a baby crying. MINNIE *stands hopelessly for a while.* ANDY *looks up.*

Here we go!

MINNIE. Andy.

ANDY. Yes.

MINNIE. Andy.

ANDY. Yes.

MINNIE. It's just.

ANDY (*puts the marking to one side*). Yes.

MINNIE. It's just, I'm feeling bad like I might have done the wrong thing.

ANDY. Right. (*Leans forward a bit.*) I see.

MINNIE. You know.

ANDY. Right. The wrong thing when?

MINNIE. Now. Yeah, now. The wrong thing now. Earlier. The wrong thing calling you.

ANDY. No, that was the right thing.

MINNIE. Yeah, I'm worried it was the wrong thing though.

ANDY. Right. Well it wasn't.

MINNIE. Okay.

They laugh.

Okay. Good.

ANDY. Okay?

MINNIE. Okay.

ANDY. Because, like I said, y'know, a few times now, I was out anyway and it was easier in actual fact, for me to nip over here, than if I'd just gone home, okay? So don't worry because I'm fine. About being here. I'm really happy about being here. Okay? You did the right thing. You heard a noise outside, it was probably a fox, you know, but you thought someone was breaking in, it's a normal reaction. For some people, okay? You did the right thing, Millie.

MINNIE. Minnie.

ANDY. Minnie! Minnie Minnie, Je-sus! I know that! It's because, I'm marking Millie's essay! Seriously, I really am, Look! (*Waves the essay about.*) Look, Millie, what's her second name – (*Checks the essay.*) Millie Sutton! Sutcliffe! Millie Sutcliffe! Millie Minnie, Millie Minnie. (*Laughs.*) So. It's all fine. You did the right thing. Your name's Minnie. We all know what we're doing.

Small silence. MINNIE *sits down.*

Brilliant.

The baby is crying upstairs.

God, that kid.

MINNIE. She's always crying.

ANDY. That's babies for you, never satisfied!

ANDY *laughs,* MINNIE *doesn't.*

MINNIE. I'm just not very good at being on my own at night.

ANDY *puts his marking to one side.*

ANDY. Well, you're not on your own now are you? I'm here!

MINNIE. It's just at night sometimes, I'm fine normally.

ANDY. Lou'll be back soon. We can all have a glass of wine. Or a cup of tea.

MINNIE. Okay.

ANDY. We can all talk about it then. If you want to. When Lou gets home.

MINNIE. I'm fine.

ANDY. Well, if you want to.

MINNIE. Okay.

They sit in silence for a bit. ANDY *checks his watch. He remains present for* MINNIE.

ANDY. You should go out maybe, with friends from university.

MINNIE *doesn't say anything.*

You must have made hundreds of friends by now. Got them all on Facebook.

MINNIE. I've always been bad at night. I feel –

ANDY. Jumpy.

MINNIE. Not really, I feel…

ANDY. A bit anxious.

MINNIE. No, well a bit. But I feel…

ANDY. Spooked.

Pause.

MINNIE. It's like my heart's beating really fast and I can't think of anything and, like, I'm trying to watch the telly or read a book and these weird thoughts barge their way into my mind. Like someone else's thoughts, sort of narrating. Do you want a cup of tea or a glass of wine now?

ANDY (*looks at his watch*). Shit, maybe she didn't catch the last Tube. (*Checks his phone.*) I'll call her. (*Calls. Waits. It goes to answerphone.*) It's gone straight to answerphone. That means she's on the Tube. That's good. She'll be here soon.

MINNIE. Okay.

ANDY. You have something, if you want.

MINNIE. I might have a cup of tea. Are you sure you don't want one?

ANDY. Oh go on then.

> MINNIE *goes into the kitchen. A moment later she appears with a half-full bottle of red wine.*

MINNIE. Or we could just finish this.

ANDY. Yeah, go on, okay…

> MINNIE *goes back into the kitchen.*

> Lou's probably just on the last Tube now.

MINNIE. Yeah.

> MINNIE *comes back over with two glasses of wine, gives one to* ANDY *and then sits down.*

ANDY. Poor old you.

MINNIE. No I'm really fine.

ANDY. Uni's great though isn't it?

MINNIE (*shifty*). It's okay.

ANDY. Just okay?

MINNIE. It's alright. I'm not massively in the mood to be honest.

ANDY. Well it's early days isn't it? Give it a couple of weeks and you'll be well in.

MINNIE. It's been a month.

ANDY. Give it a couple of months.

MINNIE. I am.

> *Pause.*

> Everyone's a bit of a knob.

ANDY. Not everyone, surely.

MINNIE. No. Probably not.

> *Pause.*

> Andy.

ANDY. Yes.

MINNIE. If I tell you something will you promise not to tell Louise?

ANDY. Ummm.

MINNIE. Sorry, I shouldn't ask you that.

MINNIE *stands up and moves to the window. She looks out.*

ANDY. No, it's just. Why can't I tell Lou?

MINNIE. Forget it, it doesn't matter. (*Looking outside.*) There's that man that lets his dog shit right in the middle of the pavement.

ANDY. I mean, of course you can tell me, if you need to. But Lou will be back any minute. She'll be on the last Tube.

MINNIE. He's doing it now. Look.

ANDY. Can it wait? Can't it be something you can tell us both?

MINNIE. Not really. Never mind though. (*Pause.*) Someone's going to step in that shit.

ANDY *gets up to look. They both stand at the window, watching.* ANDY *looks further up the road. He looks at his watch.*

ANDY. I can't really hear something from you, and in all honesty, say I'm definitely not going to tell Lou.

MINNIE. No. I know. That's fair enough.

ANDY. Is that fair enough though?

MINNIE. Yes, it is.

Pause.

ANDY (*tuts*). Now I know there's something that you need to say, it puts me in a slightly awkward situation, do you see that?

MINNIE. Yes, sorry.

ANDY. Lou is supposed to be your guardian. Type of thing.

MINNIE. She's my godmother.

ANDY. Exactly.

MINNIE. I wasn't christened, but, y'know.

ANDY. Even so. As good as.

MINNIE. Yeah.

ANDY. She's responsible for you while you're here. Sort of.

MINNIE. Yeah.

   Pause.

ANDY. You're not pregnant are you?

MINNIE. No.

ANDY. Seriously. Are you pregnant?

MINNIE. No.

ANDY. Okay. Good. Thank God for that!

   Phew! That's great. Good work.

MINNIE. Mum was supposed to give birth to me on the last day of her first-year exams.

ANDY. Wow.

MINNIE. But I was ten days late, so.

ANDY. Yeah, well she was obviously really happy to be having you, so that's a good thing, if you can make it work that's great. But for you, now, it might not be so, fortuitous.

MINNIE. Right.

ANDY. That's all I meant.

MINNIE. I see.

ANDY. Lou was at uni with someone who got pregnant, and was totally traumatised about it. Get her to tell you. Terrible situation, arsehole of a bloke, Lou had to sit up all night with this girl just to stop her giving herself an abortion with a kebab stick or something. Pissed off her head, trying to throw herself out of the window, slashing her stomach, that sort of thing. So, all I'm saying is, it's not always, you know, the best thing. (*Pause*.) But you're not. So that's okay. (*Pause*.) Yadda yadda yadda. (*Looks at his watch*.) Where the hell is she?

Pause. ANDY *looks out the window up the street. Then he moves away.* MINNIE *stays watching out the window.*

I might just wander up to the Tube actually.

MINNIE. That girl was my mum.

ANDY. What girl?

MINNIE. The pregnant throwing-herself-out-the-window girl. That would have been my mum.

ANDY. No, this was someone in Lou's year. This was in halls, Lou said she was hanging out the window of halls. That wasn't your mum! For God's – ! I'm not going to be telling you stories like that about your mum!

MINNIE. Mum was in Louise's year –

ANDY. No she wasn't –

MINNIE. She was. Mum and Louise shared a room in halls, it would definitely have been my mum.

ANDY. No, that's not right. Lou and your mum weren't, how old's your mum?

MINNIE. Thirty-nine.

ANDY. Well, how can they have been in the same year? Lou's not thirty-nine –

MINNIE. Louise is forty –

ANDY. What? –

MINNIE. Isn't she? –

ANDY (*laughing*). Don't let her hear you saying that! –

MINNIE. She was forty / in May.

ANDY. Whatever you do don't / say that in front of Lou.

MINNIE. They were in the same year, I've seen the photos with the gowns, throwing the hats –

ANDY. Lou's two years younger than me.

MINNIE. Oh. (*Pause.*) How old are you?

ANDY. Thirty-six, so.

MINNIE. Oh. Okay.

ANDY. So, you know. That wasn't your mum. And Lou's. Lou's, not, you know. That wasn't your mum.

Pause.

MINNIE. I thought they shared a room. Mum said they did. I thought.

ANDY. Well. She's wrong. Because they can't have. Can they? Unless your mum took, y'know, like, six years off, a six-year gap-year, did she?

MINNIE. No, I don't think so.

ANDY. No. (*Pause.*) I don't think so either. (*Long pause. Laughs.*) Jesus Christ, That wasn't your mum! Can you imagine? I wouldn't say a thing like that about! God! About your mum! A kebab stick! And don't tell Lou she looks forty! I don't know what's worse! She'd fucking kill herself!

ANDY*'s phone rings. He looks at caller ID.*

A-ha! (*Winks at* MINNIE *as he answers.*) Hello, young lady!… Nothing, I'm just mucking about, where are you?… Hang on, what d'y'mean?

He shoots a look at MINNIE *slightly panicked, then moves away into a corner of the room trying to be nonchalant.*

Hang on, what…

He moves again, this time into the kitchen, glancing at MINNIE *as he goes.*

Oh right… Okay, right…

MINNIE *watches him go, anxious. When left alone she lets herself panic a little, looking round the room nervously and twiddling her hair fast. She can hear* ANDY *in the kitchen saying, 'Okay,' occasionally and then ending the call.*

(*Off.*) Okay… Yes, let's speak in the morning. … No,
I'm fine… nothing, I'm fine… okay… Yes, I will, night
night, bye.

ANDY *doesn't come out straight away.* MINNIE *is very
nervous. After a long time* ANDY *re-enters. He walks
straight into the room and to the window, a brief attempt at a
jovial smile en route but clearly unsettled.*

(*Obviously feels the silence must be filled.*) Well. That's.
(*Pause, laughs uncertainly. Stops laughing. Looks out of the
window.*) No one's stepped in the –

MINNIE. Good.

ANDY. So that's good.

ANDY *makes a thing of thoroughly closing the curtains and
then turns back into the room. He stands rather hopelessly
for a moment not meeting* MINNIE*'s eye.* MINNIE *sits
anxiously waiting for him to speak.*

Well. I should probably. Are you going to be okay? If I. I
should maybe go probably.

ANDY *has a sudden flare of anger, he moves quickly to put
his work back into his bag.* MINNIE *jumps.*

I've missed the *fucking* last Tube now. Fuck *that.*

MINNIE. Sorry, I'm sorry I called you, I'm sorry I made you
come.

ANDY. Yeah, well –

MINNIE. I knew it was the wrong thing to do.

ANDY. Don't worry about it –

MINNIE. I knew it was wrong the minute I did it –

ANDY. We all make mistakes, you'll get over it.

ANDY *is stuffing all the essays into his bag, they are getting
scuffed up and caught, he can't get them in. Suddenly he
throws the bag down and sits in the chair. He never looks at*
MINNIE. MINNIE *is trying not to cry.*

MINNIE (*very quiet*). I can give you the money for a taxi.

No response.

I could go to the cashpoint.

No response.

ANDY. I expect you've known about this then have you?

MINNIE. About what? Where's Louise? What did she say?

ANDY (*very brittle, not looking at* MINNIE). Oh, she's at home, apparently. Yes, she's been in a while now. She left the meal after the first course because she had a headache, yes, terrible headache it was, just over her right temple. She got a Tube home and got in about half-nine. (*Looks at his watch.*) Yes. She took two ibruprofen and *would* have gone straight to bed but got caught up talking to you, actually. On and on you went. She stuck with it, you know, selflessly, but to be honest, she was desperate to fall into bed, not really listening, you know, what with the headache, if she's honest. She eventually got to bed about an hour ago, fell straight asleep, but then upstairs kicked off. Woke her up. She was disorientated. She was confused. Checked her phone to see what time it was and noticed my missed call. She's going back to sleep now. We'll speak in the morning. So that'll be nice.

So. The question is. The question we need to be asking ourselves. At this moment in time is. Where is Lou? If she's not here, where is she? You know. That. Is the question.

Long pause. Slowly ANDY*'s face softens, there is a moment of hope.* ANDY *gets up and quickly goes to* LOU*'s bedroom door, opens it quietly so as not to wake her and looks inside. It is empty. He returns to the chair.*

They sit in silence for a moment.

Is that what you were going to tell me earlier? The thing I couldn't tell Lou?

MINNIE. No! No, nothing like that.

ANDY. Yeah, sure.

MINNIE. It wasn't about Louise –

ANDY. This happens a lot then does it? You on your own at night a lot are you?

MINNIE. Sometimes. Not a lot. Just when she's staying at yours...

ANDY. She never stays at mine.

MINNIE. Oh. Well, I didn't know whether. / I thought she was at yours.

ANDY. She never stays at mine. So that's, interesting.

MINNIE. Andy, she'll just be staying at a friend's, she'll have decided to crash at a friend's. Because of the headache. / Don't jump to –

ANDY. What headache? She hasn't fucking got a headache has she?

MINNIE. You don't know that.

ANDY. Minnie. Look. It's not your. Sorry, I'm sorry I shouted. I'm sorry you're dragged into all this. It's nothing to do with you, okay? Why don't you just go to bed. Go to bed, yeah? You've got school, not school, you know, college, in the morning.

MINNIE. I feel bad leaving you. It's all my fault you're here.

ANDY. Don't be silly, I'm fine. I'm *fine*. Go to bed, I don't need babysitting, I'm a big grown-up man, I'm not going to do anything stupid. It's all okay.

MINNIE. She's probably just at a friend's house –

ANDY. Yeah. It's okay.

MINNIE. You know, she probably said that because she didn't want you to worry! Please, Andy, don't be angry with her. I think there is definitely a really good explanation for this. It's my fault, she probably couldn't face coming back home and having to talk to me. I'm doing her head in. She'd be too kind to say she had a headache, I know I talk about things too much, I would probably try and talk to her. Like she said. (*Pause.*) Andy. Please.

ANDY. She said she *had* been talking to you. She said she was *here*. (*Gestures hopelessly to the room, empty of* LOU.)

MINNIE. Maybe she was disorientated because she'd just woken up.

ANDY. It's okay, Minnie, go to bed.

Silence.

Je-sus, I can't believe I've let this happen to me *again*. I swore, I promised myself, never again. How can this have happened? What is it about me that allows people to treat me with such, I'm a good person, I don't deserve this, this, this. Disregard.

MINNIE (*hovering, helpless*). Oh God.

ANDY. How has this happened? Hey? How. Has this happened?

MINNIE. Nothing's happened.

ANDY. You have to admit though, right, it's not looking good. Y'know, if she's not here, where is she? If she's not here, right...

MINNIE. I really think everything's going to be okay –

ANDY. You've got to watch your back, you know, that's my advice to you. Watch. Your. Back. Cos no other fucker's watching it for you, d'y'know what I mean? Ten years ago, fuck me, no, it's more than that, sixteen years ago, sixteen years! I learnt that lesson. I thought I was taught that lesson loud and clear from Justine Mercer. But no, here I am again, learning it a-fucking-gain. I'm going to tell you this, Minnie, I'm going to tell you this story to stop you from falling into... (*Takes a breath and starts speaking very fast.*) When I was your age, younger than you, when I was fifteen, I started going out with a girl from school, it was amazing, really serious, and as time went on, a year, two years, we got stronger and more, solid, and I knew, I really felt like we were going to be together for ever. (*Hits the side of his head.*) Fucking idiot! And she felt like that too, we knew everyone thought we were kids, they said, 'How can you know?' But we did. We loved each other, it was real. I can't believe I'm telling you this. Why am I telling you this? Anyway, so we finished school, and she wanted us to go to university together, you know, the same university, and the course she wanted to do was at Essex, in Colchester, an engineering thing. I wanted to be an architect, always had, right from when I was. There wasn't an architecture course at Essex, there might be now, I don't know, but then there wasn't, anyway. But, I wanted to be with her and so I put all that on hold and applied to Essex to do a history degree. I liked history, you know, I was good at it, it wasn't some random, y'know. And we went there, and got a double room in a sort of couples' block, the rooms were poky, mostly foreign students, lots of East African students, for some reason, if I remember rightly, and we were living together for the first time, y'know, it was… too much. Probably. Anyway. She was doing her engineering, and I was doing my history and she got really into her course and started socialising with different mates and I, well I didn't really, click, with that many people on mine, I mean I did make friends, I wasn't like some Billy No Mates, obviously, but I just wanted to be with her, I wasn't looking so far outside of that. Stupidly. Y'know. It was stupid. All the wrong thing, obviously, anyone can see that. They did! Everyone said it was crazy, to shut down opportunities like that. I wanted to be an architect!

MINNIE. Did you split up?

ANDY. Halfway through the third term she got pregnant. We were only nineteen. It wasn't what we had. Intended.

MINNIE. Right.

ANDY. You're not interested in all this. I just had to tell you the background, to make the, the next point –

MINNIE. No, no.

ANDY. You probably haven't been to Colchester, I don't know if you know it, but it's a bit of a dive, back then it was, I don't know, they might have improved it now, but back then it was a bit. Grim. We got a couple of rooms at the top of this house and I jacked in my course and got a shitty job in a shitty factory, and in a sweatshop warehouse, I gave *everything* up, all my dreams for myself, all my… And Justine Mercer carried on with her course. Oh yes. And then. About a month before the baby was due she told me. She told me, it wasn't mine. Well, she said it was more likely not to be mine. 'I don't think it's yours.' You know, there was another guy. Some twat. A bloke on her course in the year above. A rugby player. Anyway. Yadda yadda yadda.

Long pause.

MINNIE. I thought you said university was brilliant.

ANDY. Listen, Minnie. Sorry, this has all turned into something else. The point I am trying to make, you have to, people aren't necessarily. You know, if you've got a boyfriend –

MINNIE. I haven't got a boyfriend so –

ANDY. Yeah, but what I'm trying to say is, don't assume people are, y'know, because basically, people are *not* looking out for you.

MINNIE. Well, sometimes they are.

ANDY. Sometimes, though. They're not. And that. Is my point.

Silence. ANDY *stares into space.*

MINNIE. Did you see her again?

ANDY. About three years ago I saw her in a service station near my parents' house. Standing there, on the phone.

MINNIE. With the child?

ANDY. On her own, I recognised her instantly, from the back of her head actually, I knew her.

MINNIE. Did she recognise you?

ANDY. She didn't see me.

Pause.

MINNIE. It's not too late for you to –

ANDY. Of course it is…

MINNIE. You could still be an architect.

ANDY. I did go back and finish my degree, by the way, just in case you. I don't want you thinking I'm not, qualified, to teach… (*Gestures to the scrumpled-up essays on the floor.*)

MINNIE. What if she had pretended it wasn't your baby –

ANDY. And I went back and took an MA, some time later, so –

MINNIE. What if she was saying it wasn't your baby to save you from throwing your dreams of being an architect away?

ANDY. Why would she do that?

MINNIE. If she really loved you. She might have said it to set you free.

ANDY. No.

MINNIE. She might. (*Pause*.) You might have a sixteen-year-old son or daughter somewhere.

ANDY. It wasn't like that.

MINNIE. You don't know.

ANDY. I do. It wasn't like that. People don't do things like that.

MINNIE. I think they do. I think people are basically good.

ANDY. Yeah? Wait till you're my age –

MINNIE. I think people are good if they can be.

ANDY. Wait until you've loved someone, and trusted someone, and planned your life around someone. My mum's storing a fridge freezer in my Uncle Alan's fucking garage, for fuck's sake. Me and Lou are supposed to be moving in together this year. You know? This is serious stuff.

Pause.

The other night as well, she said to me, 'I'm knackered, I'm going straight to sleep,' I said to her, 'I'll come round, we can chill out, whatever, be together,' she's saying, 'No, I'll be asleep.' Fuck's sake, I haven't even got a key any more, you've got my key. If I'd had a key, I could have just let myself in, it wouldn't matter if she was asleep, you know, that's what I used to do. Before. (*Starts to cry*.) What's she doing this for? Why's she doing this to me? Why's she throwing it all away? I can't bear it, I can't bear to lose her. I can't start again.

MINNIE *moves next to him, puts her hand on* ANDY*'s arm, passes him his glass of wine.*

MINNIE. Andy. Listen to me.

ANDY. I'm not being funny but, you know, you've got my key.

MINNIE. This is what's happened. You've woken her up, she was disorientated, she'll wake up in the morning in a strange bed and think, hang on! Where am I? You'll have a laugh about it, you'll say, 'You said you were at home! I was at your flat!' All this, you'll laugh about it.

ANDY. You know, it was okay before. When I had a key.

MINNIE. There, you see. I've got a good feeling about it all. Louise is a good person,

ANDY. Is she? Do you think?

MINNIE. I know she is, I've known her my whole life. She has always been so good to me. And my mum. Such a loyal, true friend. I know that she is good at heart. Okay? And here – (*Finds her house keys in her bag*.) I'm going to leave these out tonight and first thing in the morning I'll get them copied. And then. You can have your keys back. Okay? It's all going to be alright again. Please don't be upset, Andy, please be happy, please be happy again.

There is a knock at the door to the flat. A quiet, polite knock. MINNIE *and* ANDY *freeze. Silence. Another knock.*

ANDY (*whispered*). What the fuck?

MINNIE. Who is it?

ANDY. It's upstairs, it has to be, they're in the, the, communal space. They're in the hall.

MINNIE. Shall I open it?

ANDY. No. Stay here.

MINNIE. Shall I just ask who it is?

ANDY. Shhh. Don't do anything. They'll go away.

Another knock. ANDY *and* MINNIE *stay absolutely still.*

MINNIE. Please let's answer it. They might be. They might need help.

ANDY. Shhh. Come here.

There is the sound of a baby crying very close, as if directly outside the door. MINNIE *instinctively moves towards the door.* ANDY *holds her back, they look at each other.*

MINNIE. Please let me answer it, Andy.

ANDY. No. (*Pause.*) No way. Definitely not.

MINNIE. I think I know what it is.

ANDY. No. It's nothing to do with you.

The sound of the main front door closing. ANDY *looks out of the window.*

See. It's her, the woman. She's gone up towards the main road.

MINNIE. Is she okay?

ANDY. Fuck knows, who cares?

MINNIE. Does she look alright? (*Looks out the window.*)

ANDY (*moving back into the room*). Do not get involved. Rule number, lesson number one. Hang on to your own, your own hat, or whatever the thing is. Lesson number two, look after number one. It is not your job to look after everyone else. Do you hear me, Minnie? Seriously. It will cause you less heartache in the long run if you learn these lessons now. It will prepare you for adult life, it will keep your heart intact. Okay? Got that?

MINNIE. Yes.

ANDY. Good girl. (*Sits down.*) I'm okay. You don't have to worry about me. I'm fine.

ANDY *puts his head in his hands.* MINNIE *watches out the window.*

You haven't got that photo, have you, the graduation one with your mum and –

MINNIE. Not here, no. It's at home. It's on my wall. I can get it if you like. / Bring it back down with me when I –

ANDY. No, no, it's okay, it's probably not / relevant.

MINNIE. Okay.

ANDY. It's fine. *Phooooh.* (*Big blowing-out-of-stress noise.*)
I'm fine now. Don't you worry about all that. Sorry about
that. Little outburst there.

*ANDY gestures to the essays. He starts to gather them up
neatly and put them in his bag. MINNIE watches him.*

MINNIE. I won't forget about the key.

ANDY. That was Justine, Lou's not Justine. I have to move on.
Thanks, Minnie. You are so right about the disorientated
thing, the friend's house, the headache and all that. Y'know,
let's pretend this never happened, let's erase. Let's delete
that. Okay?

MINNIE. Okay.

ANDY. Let's say I was never… okay? And you never… okay?
Blah blah blah.

ANDY gathers his stuff, puts on his coat.

You don't need to mention the whole misunderstanding thing
to Lou, okay? And in return I won't say anything about you
calling me all the way over here for nothing, y'know, all that
silly fuss about the fox.

Beat.

MINNIE. Okay.

ANDY. Have we got a deal?

MINNIE. Yes.

ANDY. Good stuff.

*ANDY stands in the middle of the room in his coat. MINNIE
looks at him.*

Lou is a good person.

MINNIE. She has a good heart.

ANDY. She does. I know she does.

*Sound of people arguing upstairs, doors slamming, a baby
crying.*

Blackout.

Four

Lights up on LOU*'s sitting room. Night. There is a baby, about ten months old, asleep on the sofa under a blanket.* LOU *is standing, very agitated and panicky.* ANDY *lets himself in with a key. He is carrying his work bag and a pack of nappies. He comes over to the sofa. They look at the baby and speak so as not to wake it.*

ANDY. I can't believe she just –

LOU. I told you, I told you on the phone –

ANDY. And she didn't say how long she'd be? She just –

LOU. She said she'd be twenty fucking minutes and that was at quarter to five. That was four fucking hours ago.

ANDY. Have you phoned the police?

LOU. Of course not, don't be stupid, yeah, cos that would go down really well –

ANDY. Have you got any food for it? Or a bottle or something?

LOU. *No!* She said she'd be twenty minutes… this is a *nightmare*, I've had to cancel a whole load of stuff –

ANDY. Right. Phone the police.

LOU. Stop saying that, I am not going to do that –

ANDY. What did she say?

LOU. I told you, she was crying hysterically, she kept going on about Minnie, 'Where's Minnie? Where's Minnie?' She practically threw the baby at me –

ANDY. I can't believe you let her in –

LOU. I didn't let her in, *I* wasn't in, she was just in the hall when I got back from work, she was hysterical, I didn't have time to –

ANDY. What's she talking about Minnie for?

LOU. I don't know. I don't know what the hell is going on. Something is. Something has been happening. Minnie's been doing something. Weird. She was hanging around the other

night, hovering about while I was getting ready to go out.
Wanting to *talk*. Fucking hell, if she's got involved with the
fucking *junkie* upstairs. Encouraging her in some way. I'm
going to have to send her back to Mel. I can't be expected to
cope with this. Not on top of everything else.

ANDY. Okay. / Calm down.

LOU. I can't be expected to take this on, she's *damaged*, you
know, she's going to attract. She's like a damage magnet –

ANDY. Okay.

LOU. It's like her dysfunction is giving off some sort of scent,
chaos is following her in off the street.

ANDY. Oh God.

LOU. And *now*, this is a *whole* baby, you know. On my sofa.

ANDY. I'm going to phone the police because this is too far –

ANDY *takes out his mobile*, LOU *flies across the room and
grabs it off him*, ANDY *tries to get it back off her, they
grapple with it.*

LOU. Give me it –

ANDY. For Christ's sake, you stupid girl –

LOU. Why won't you listen to me, you never hear a single
thing I say –

ANDY. I hear you, it's crazy. A hysterical junkie dumps her
baby on you and you won't phone the police, I've never
heard anything so ridiculous, she might never come back,
then what?

LOU *has the phone. They stop fighting.*

Jesus. Christ.

The baby stirs.

LOU (*really loudly*). Shhhh.

Long pause.

(*Calmly.*) Of course she'll come back, she lives upstairs.
She's obviously going to come back.

ANDY. Oh yes well. Obviously. (*Pause*.) Because let's face it. In all other aspects of her life she does exactly what you might expect. So. Y'know. Hey.

Silence.

LOU. I left you about ten messages. Where have you been?

ANDY. At work. (*He obviously hasn't.*)

LOU. Till now?

ANDY. Till about forty minutes ago, yeah.

LOU. How come?

ANDY *has run out of steam with the lying. He looks worried.*

Where have you really been?

ANDY *sits carefully next to the baby. He leans back. He leans forward and puts his head in his hands.*

What are you lying for? You can't lie. What are you trying to lie for?

ANDY. I really don't need this.

LOU. What? (*Pause*.) For God's sake, Andy. What?

ANDY (*looks at* LOU *for a moment*). Okay.

LOU. What?

ANDY (*a moment*). Firstly let me assure you that *absolutely nothing* is as it seems. There's a couple of stuff I haven't told you recently, and don't get angry, I thought I was doing the right thing, I didn't want you jumping to the wrong conclusions because I can assure you –

LOU. Just tell me.

ANDY. Okay.

ANDY *doesn't say anything.*

LOU. Go on then.

ANDY. Okay. Do you remember me telling you about a girl I went out with at university called / Justine?

LOU. Justine. Justine Mercer, yes.

ANDY. Justine Mercer, that's right. Okay.

LOU. She had it off with a footballer / and got pregnant.

ANDY. A rugby player –

LOU. Right, whatever. Justine Mercer.

ANDY. Yes. Well. Justine Mercer and I are. Justine Mercer and I got back in touch! On Facebook actually.

LOU. Right. Well that's nice. Is it nice?

Pause.

Is it, sorry, is that it?

ANDY. Okay. So Justine and I got back in touch on Facebook. Initially, okay. And then Justine and I had a brief chat on the phone.

LOU. Right. This is like a book for early readers. Just tell me.

ANDY. I think I've *possibly* got a sixteen-year-old daughter. So.

LOU *stares.*

So. That's the point. I've been trying to make.

LOU *laughs.*

Okay.

LOU *stops laughing.*

Should we be worried this baby's just sleeping? Like this.

LOU. You and Justine Mercer have got a sixteen-year-old daughter?

ANDY. Possibly. It's a possibility. That we have.

LOU. It's a possibility that she exists? Or it's a possibility that she's yours? Sorry, sorry, *what*?

ANDY. No, no, she exists. I knew you'd be like this. She exists, of course, she exists. She got pregnant when I was with her. I just don't have confirmation that she's, y'know, there's no actual confirmation vis-à-vis the actual DNA testing of the child.

LOU. And no one thought to mention anything until now?

ANDY. I thought she was definitely not mine. I didn't know there was a possibility...

LOU. How can *you* be a father? (*Laughs. Bursts into tears.*)

ANDY. Lou. Come on. It's *fine* though. (*Goes to her.*) This is not going to affect *us*, okay? In no way is this going to affect you and me.

LOU. This is really, this really is, like, the biggest lie –

ANDY. No. No, it's not a lie.

LOU. What is it then? / You've kept it from me.

ANDY. I knew you'd take it like this. Jesus, this isn't about you, okay? I had no idea, I hadn't even thought about Justine Mercer for *years*. This is nothing to do with *us*. For fuck's sake. I need you to support me here.

LOU. Why did you contact her then? If you haven't thought about her for years, why did you suddenly decide to contact her?

ANDY. I just. I just, it was something someone said. About the child. It was.

LOU. Who? Who said something?

ANDY. God, I don't know, Lou, I can't remember now –

LOU. You must remember, who were you talking to about the child?

ANDY. Just some girl, I don't know, it got me thinking, that's the important thing, it doesn't matter who it was, does it?

LOU. Some girl? What are you talking about? What girl?

ANDY. Just some. *I don't know!* Stop asking me all these questions! I'm in the middle of it here, y'know. I don't even know if the child is mine or not, this might all be a total, dead end for nothing. Jesus, *Lou*! I come here, desperate for some love and support and there's a fucking, a fucking junkie's baby on the sofa and you're behaving like the fucking Gestapo. Give me a break!

Silence. The baby stirs.

LOU *goes into the kitchen, sound of fridge opening and closing. A text message beeps on her phone on the table.*

ANDY *stares ahead.*

LOU *re-enters. She is totally calm and okay.*

LOU. What do babies eat?

ANDY. Bananas? Mashed up.

LOU. Oh yes. (*Pause.*) Well. I've got a banana.

Pause.

So you met up with Justine Mercer did you?

ANDY. Yes, we met up. (*Gestures vaguely beyond the front door.*) We met up, just for a, we met up just now.

LOU. What was it like seeing her? Was it weird?

ANDY. A bit.

LOU. Has she changed?

ANDY. Not really. A bit. She looks. She's not twenty any more.

LOU. No. None of us are.

ANDY. So, you feel okay about it now, do you? You understand why I didn't mention it before?

LOU. Yes. I feel okay about it. Yes, I do.

ANDY. Good. Great. (*Pause.*) I just had to know. Once the seed was sown in my mind.

LOU *laughs.*

For want of a better. I just had to know. And, you know, what will be will be. If she does turn out to be mine, well you know, that will be the next, the next, the next bridge. If you like. That I have to cross.

LOU. Okay, Andy. Well that's good.

ANDY. Yes. It's the right thing. To do.

Pause.

I'm sorry I didn't tell you about it.

Pause.

Lou?

LOU. What?

ANDY. I said, I'm sorry. I didn't tell you. Sorry about not telling you about the possible daughter, thing.

LOU. I know.

ANDY. I just need you to be with me on this. I need you to understand.

Pause.

That I didn't lie to you, I just made the decision not to tell you something that I didn't know would necessarily be of any significance. At that time.

ANDY *moves to her and touches her.*

I might be a dad!

Silence. Nothing from LOU.

For fuck's sake, Lou, can you just.

LOU (*away from him*). I don't think I want to be with you any more.

ANDY. What?

LOU (*turning to him, gentle*). Not just because of this, I've been, you know it hasn't been right for a while –

ANDY. When? It's fine, it's good, don't fucking do this –

LOU. We've stopped communicating –

ANDY. Who has? Lou. Look / at me.

LOU. You didn't tell me a whole major thing, Andy. / It just confirms –

ANDY. It wasn't a major thing, there must be loads of things that you don't tell me –

LOU. An increasing distance between us –

ANDY. In fact, actually, if we're talking about this –

LOU. It's not working any more. / It's not just about Justine Mercer, this has been coming for ages, please, Andy.

ANDY. It is working, you can't just decide / that's it's not –

LOU. It's not working for me –

ANDY. Like what? –

LOU. Loads of things, / a whole list of things.

ANDY. You can't think of anything.

LOU. Please, Andy. It's dead.

ANDY. What?

LOU. Stop trying to / resuscitate it.

ANDY. What are you saying all this for?

LOU. I'm doing the right thing. It's what I feel.

ANDY. Can we just. This bloody baby. Have you buzzed upstairs? Is there anyone else in?

LOU. There's no one up there.

ANDY. Have you rung the buzzer?

LOU. There's no one there.

ANDY. Lou. Listen to me. This is crazy. You've got this all wrong. Don't make this about *you*. I just needed to find out for myself. Please. You're tired, and shocked / and the baby's here and.

LOU. I'm not shocked actually –

ANDY. The headaches, it's all getting on top of you. Let's get out of here, we can have a drink…

LOU. The baby's here, you idiot. I can't go out can I?

ANDY. Okay. Are you seeing someone else?

LOU (*looks directly at* ANDY). No!

ANDY. Because, y'know, there have been a couple of times, there was this one night actually / when.

LOU. No. What the fuck is this? You're the one with the secret chats on Facebook, and the cosy little reunions with your stupid, promiscuous ex. Okay, you want the details. Okay then. I feel *stuck*. I feel anxious all the time. I feel *panicked* when I see you, I'm not pleased to hear your voice, when I pick up an answer-machine message from you, my heart feels *flat* and *hard*. You *irritate* me, the slightest thing, the way you do that circular movement with your hand when you describe feelings, makes me, I feel *repulsed* actually, I know that sounds extreme, but it is *repulsion*. I don't want this. I don't recognise myself any more. I am floating in between feelings I used to have, and feelings I am prevented from having by being with you. I am *dead* with you. Just the *thought* of being beyond this makes me feel lighter. Please. Let me end this. I am suspended here, wanting to drop back into my life, and. Being. Prevented.

ANDY. I have never prevented you from doing a single thing –

LOU. Not literally, okay. / It's not just that.

ANDY. When have I ever prevented you from doing something?

LOU. Andy! I'm finishing with you. Okay? People break up all the time! They need different things. They realise, I have realised. I have realised I absolutely, don't want this relationship. With you. Now.

Pause.

ANDY. Right.

LOU. Y'know, I *thought* I did. I *did* in fact. But now I don't.

ANDY. I see.

LOU. Sorry.

ANDY. Yeah, right.

LOU. I am. I am sorry. It's not. Your fault.

ANDY. Well, you know, it must be a bit my fault. If I'm not offering you what you need any more. / That's a bit my fault.

LOU. Okay, well, I don't even know what I want you to offer me / I can't expect you to know.

ANDY. Well, that's the difficulty.

LOU. Yes.

ANDY. I do try. / My hardest to –

LOU. I know you do.

ANDY. Accommodate you / I have *tried* to offer you –

LOU. I don't want you to accommodate me.

ANDY. – what you *appear* to need.

> LOU *silent*.

> And I'm sorry if I haven't been the person you needed me to be. (*Pause*.) Y'know, who do you need me to be? Then.

> *Pause,* LOU *silent*.

> Because if you tell me, then I could try to be. That person.

> LOU *is silent*.

> Right! (*Gets up*.) What to do about this baby.

> ANDY *and* LOU *look at the baby*.

> It's breathing heavily. Is it supposed to do that?

LOU. It's probably been drugged.

ANDY. Has it been asleep the whole time?

LOU. No, it screamed for hours. It fell asleep just before you came. That's why I was so desperate. I didn't know how to shut it up, I had to put it in the kitchen and shut the door, it just screamed and screamed.

ANDY. Right. Well let's move it somewhere out the way.

LOU. What for? It's fine where it is.

ANDY. We can't sit down / it's taking up the whole sofa.

LOU. What do you need to sit down for, aren't you going?

> ANDY *looks at* LOU.

Aren't you though? What is there to stay for? Andy? We're
finished aren't we? We're done.

ANDY *looks at* LOU.

I thought we just said.

ANDY *looks at* LOU.

What?

ANDY *looks at* LOU. LOU *looks back at him and then looks
away, embarrassed.* ANDY *moves towards the baby and
gently gathers it up.*

Put it in Minnie's room then. On the bed, close to the wall.

ANDY *carries the baby into* MINNIE*'s room.* LOU *reads
her text message. She panics.*

LOU *goes to the window, looks out, back to the sofa, sits,
stands. She starts to text but stops when* ANDY *returns.*

ANDY *is holding a photograph in his hand.*

Okay. I really think you should just go now, Andy.

ANDY. I need to ask you something.

LOU. We've said everything, okay? What's the point in
prolonging things? In a week, or a couple of weeks we could
meet up, you know, see how things are then maybe.

ANDY. I haven't said everything I want to say. I need to ask
you something.

ANDY *holds up the photograph. It is the graduation photo.*

LOU. What are you doing with that?

ANDY. Is this you, yeah?

LOU. What are you fiddling about in Minnie's room for?
Looking at her stuff. / Put it back.

ANDY. Is this you and Minnie's mum? I will put it back. Okay.
Just answer the question.

LOU (*laughing*). What are you talking about? It's not *Midsomer
Murders.* I want you to go, Andy.

ANDY. Just, yes or no? Okay? It's not difficult. Is this you? Graduating with Mel? What's the problem?

LOU (*laughing*). For fuck's sake.

ANDY. Why are you laughing?

LOU. Listen to yourself.

ANDY. Why are you laughing?

LOU. You've gone mad.

ANDY. Is this your graduation?

LOU. *Yes!* Probably. I can't see it properly. Put it back!

ANDY. Stop laughing.

LOU (*laughing*). I'm not. Will you just go home. To your home.

ANDY. Why did you freak out that time in Lisbon when I was looking at your passport?

LOU. What? Are these questions connected?

ANDY. Yes, they're fucking connected.

LOU. Fucking go home!

ANDY (*pushes the photograph roughly into her face*). Can you see it properly now? Fucking answer the question.

LOU *snatches the photograph and rips it up.* LOU *throws the pieces onto the sofa and looks straight at* ANDY.

Answer the question.

LOU. I fucking will if you've got the balls to ask it –

ANDY. How Old Are You?

LOU. Forty. I'm forty. Is that what you want? Now fuck off out of my flat.

Silence.

ANDY. You *bitch*.

LOU. Yeah? You don't know the half of it –

ANDY. I would have spent my *life* with you.

LOU. Well, lucky me –

ANDY. I would have had kids with you, / I would have –

LOU. Yeah? And now you've had kids with Justine Mercer so / fucking yippee-doo for you.

ANDY. – loved you till I took my. Last breath. I would have. Fucking. You could have had *all* of me. You stayed with my parents. Making them think that this was something *real*. You. Stupid. Stupid. *Old*.

ANDY and LOU stare at each other.

Silence.

The buzzer on the front door goes.

LOU closes her eyes and stays where she is. Full of dread and resignation.

I'll get it, you get the baby.

ANDY goes out to the front door.

LOU stays where she is.

After a moment ANDY returns with KARL.

Come through. The mother said she'd be twenty minutes, mate. That was hours ago. Like four hours ago. You know. We really don't need this.

LOU. He's nothing to do with the baby. (*To* KARL.) Hi.

KARL. Alright.

LOU (*to* KARL). I got your text.

KARL. Right. You didn't text back to say not to come / so.

LOU. I'm really sorry about your dad.

KARL. Yeah.

LOU. I really am so sorry.

KARL. Yes. He.

ANDY. Sorry, who are you then?

LOU. This is Karl. / Andy. Karl.

ANDY. Hi, Karl.

ANDY and KARL shake hands.

Sorry, I thought you had come for the kid. That we've got. In the room, there. But you haven't. Okay.

ANDY is looking to LOU for help.

LOU (*very half-hearted*). I work with Karl, I've told you about Karl, Andy. He works at. He works at, work.

ANDY. Does he?

LOU (*to ANDY*). Karl's dad has just. Passed away. (*To KARL.*) I'm so sorry.

LOU looks briefly at ANDY.

ANDY. Right.

LOU goes to KARL and puts her arms around him. She holds him for a few moments. ANDY watches.

(*To LOU.*) What, he's literally just died? This minute?

LOU. Yes, Andy. Okay?

ANDY (*to LOU*). And you two know each other from work?

LOU. Yes.

KARL (*to LOU*). Shall I go? Would it be easier if I went?

LOU. It would be easier yes. I don't think I'm doing easier tonight, so.

ANDY (*to LOU*). What am I looking at here? What is this? Is this? Yeah?

LOU. Karl's dad just died, Andy. He's just lost his dad.

KARL (*to LOU*). I was just at the hospital, I was literally walking past the end of your road.

LOU (*to KARL*). It's fine. Sit down. Do you want a drink?

KARL. I'll just. Can I smoke in here?

LOU. Of course you can.

ANDY. Fucking. What?

KARL *sits on the sofa and starts to build a spliff.*

LOU. I'll get you an ashtray.

LOU *goes into the kitchen. We hear her struggling with the back door.* ANDY *stares at* KARL.

ANDY *looks to the kitchen, and then back to* KARL.

ANDY. I know now's probably not the time but. I need to make some sense of this.

KARL. I was just passing the end of the street, mate. (*Stands. Searching for a lighter in his pockets.*) This other stuff is between you and Lou.

ANDY. Okay and you're having a. A. Thing? Is that correct?

KARL. Whatever, mate. That's for you and Lou to sort out, d'y'know what I'm saying?

LOU *re-enters with an ashtray. She gives it to* KARL. *He puts it down.*

I'm going to split.

LOU. No, don't go. / Stay here.

KARL. Nah you're alright. It's too weird. This is doing my head in.

ANDY. Oh it's doing *your* head in?

LOU. Where are you going to go?

KARL. I'm cool, don't worry about me.

LOU. I don't want you to go.

KARL. Whatever. You've got shit you need to sort, yeah?

LOU *looks at* ANDY. *He is just staring at her.*

LOU. It's sorted. (*Pause.*) It's sorted, isn't it, Andy?

ANDY. Is it?

LOU. Isn't it?

ANDY. I don't know.

LOU. Andy.

ANDY. I don't know what the fuck is going on. In front of my eyes. I don't know how all this is happening. Y'know. What the *fuck*? Are you playing at?

KARL *lights his spliff and makes a move to go*.

LOU. Hang on! Don't. Stay there a minute. (*To* ANDY.) His dad just died, Andy, please.

ANDY. I fucking know! I'm fucking sorry, okay? What do you want me to say?

KARL (*to* LOU). See you later, alright? / Laters okay?

LOU. Wait! (*Holds onto* KARL.) I want to be there for you. Please.

ANDY. Oh my God, this is *unreal*. What? (*Looks at his watch*.) In the last, in the last, two and a half hours, my life has, *exploded* into thousands of tiny pieces. Everything, I thought I knew has been pulled from under my feet. And now I'm not even allowed to. (*To* KARL.) Any, any, *anger*, I might want to direct towards you is, *insignificant* in the light of your, your…

KARL. Shit.

KARL *hands the spliff to* LOU. *He moves away and sits on the sofa*. LOU *smokes*.

ANDY. Don't smoke that.

LOU. I can smoke what I like.

ANDY. What are you smoking that for?

LOU *takes long defiant drags*.

I'm trying to talk to you, I'm trying to have a conversation.

LOU. Talk to me then.

ANDY. Jesus Christ, *Lou*. Is this what it's come to? Has it come to this? I feel like my life's been *torn* from me. Who are you? Who the hell *are* you? Standing there, the collapse of our lives, a mere, a tiny *insignificance*. (*Lets his anger flood into his words*.) Making *me* feel bad for not telling you that I contacted my ex on *Facebook* –

LOU. Oh and had a *child* with her.

ANDY. I know what you've been doing, / I'm not *stupid*.

LOU. And had a *child* with her.

ANDY. Headaches and early nights for, oh my God, I don't know how long, you've been *fucking* some *bloke*.

ANDY moves close to LOU suddenly, as if he could strike her. KARL stands up instinctively.

Oh yeah, that's right, here he is. Wearing his dad's death like a riot shield. Honest to God, mate, I would *so* like to lay in to you.

KARL (*very easy, effortless, unaggressive tone*). Fucking bring it on, you cock.

The door to the flat opens and MINNIE enters. She walks in to a shocked silence.

MINNIE. Oh sorry!

LOU. Hi! It's Minnie!

MINNIE. Hi, sorry.

LOU. Don't be sorry, it's fine, come in, come in, it's all fine here. We're all just having a. Talk. Come in, close the door, in you come. Okay?

LOU has had the spliff hidden behind her back, she hands it back to KARL. MINNIE comes in. Wary, looking at everyone. Trying not to take up any space.

MINNIE. Hi. Hi, Andy.

ANDY. Hi.

LOU. And this is Karl, Minnie.

MINNIE. Hi, Karl.

KARL. Alright.

LOU. He's a. His dad's actually just died so he's. A bit sad.

MINNIE. Oh God.

LOU. Very sad. Obviously.

MINNIE. Yes. (*Pause.*) How terrible. (*Pause.*) I'm so sorry.

KARL *nods*.

Silence. KARL *sits back down on the sofa and starts to build another spliff while still smoking the lit one*.

LOU. So! That's great!

MINNIE. I'm just going to go to bed I think, I'm really knackered, so. I'll just get a glass of water if that's okay and.

LOU. Oh right. Oh actually, there's just. There's kind of a *baby* on your bed. Sorry about that, it's just the baby? From upstairs? I know it sounds mad, it's a long sort of story, but it's there.

MINNIE. Mary?

LOU. Mary?

MINNIE. Karen's baby?

LOU. Karen? The junkie's baby, upstairs?

MINNIE. Yes, Mary.

LOU. Right. Because I was going to ask you about that actually.

MINNIE. Have you been looking after Mary this evening?

LOU. Well, kind of. Have you looked after her before, then?

ANDY *starts gathering his stuff aggressively*.

ANDY. Fuck this.

LOU. We'll talk about it another time.

MINNIE. Yes sorry. So Mary's on my bed.

LOU. Yes.

ANDY. Right. I'm out of here.

LOU. Oh okay, Andy, well.

ANDY. Is that all you can say?

LOU. Well.

Pause.

ANDY. Go on.

LOU *starts laughing*

LOU. Sorry. I'm not laughing.

ANDY. You are laughing.

LOU. I'm not, sorry, sorry. (*Managing to stop laughing.*)

ANDY. Is that all you can do? You, you *child*.

LOU *starts laughing again.*

LOU. It's just! Can't anyone else see the funny side? This is *ridiculous*! Isn't it?

No one else can see the funny side.

Oh my dear God! Fuck this! Karl, give me that.

LOU *takes the spliff off* KARL. LOU *physically suddenly relaxes, lets go somehow. She sweeps to the sofa switching on a music system en route. The music comes on loudly. She dances for a few seconds before throwing herself onto the sofa next to* KARL.

MINNIE *is looking around trying to assess the situation.*

She sees KARL *and* LOU *sitting together on the sofa not looking at anyone.*

She sees ANDY *standing hopeless.*

She sees the ripped photograph of her mum's graduation.

ANDY (*over the music*). So you have nothing to say to me? Nothing? Is that right?

LOU. Jesus Christ! Somebody help me!

MINNIE *makes a definite decision. She takes off her coat and goes into the kitchen and fills and switches on the kettle.*

(*Over the music*.) Oh Andy Andy Andy! What can I say? The mask has fallen. I'm revealed. What can I say! You have uncovered the truth!

MINNIE *returns*.

I'm the Incredible Hulk!

MINNIE *picks up the packet of nappies*.

MINNIE. These are for Mary are they?

LOU. Yes, Andy bought them! (*Laughing*.)

MINNIE. Has anyone changed her recently?

LOU *looks blank*.

Right.

MINNIE *exits into her bedroom*.

ANDY (*over the music*). I'm going to go now, Lou. And that will be that. This will be over. This is how the last three years is going to end. And you're happy with that are you?

LOU. I wouldn't say I was happy with it, no. But. *C'est la vie*.

ANDY. My God.

MINNIE *comes out of her room with a baby's bottle and some formula in a tin and goes into the kitchen*.

MINNIE. She's asleep. She's safe and well. Right.

LOU. Where did you get that from?

Over the dialogue, MINNIE *multitasks: preparing tea, sterilising the bottle with boiling water, preparing a feed*.

MINNIE. Who wants tea? Andy?

ANDY. I am going home.

MINNIE. Right. I think that's sensible. Do you want me to call you a cab?

ANDY. No thank you. I'll get the Tube.

MINNIE. Okay. Louise? Tea?

LOU. Darling! You've turned into Miss Tiggy-Winkle.

MINNIE. Do you want tea though?

LOU. You need a little pinny.

KARL. I'll have a tea if you're making one.

MINNIE. I am.

LOU. Oh, Min! You've got a customer for your little tea shop!

MINNIE. How do you take your tea, Karl?

KARL. Milk two sugars please.

MINNIE. Coming up.

LOU. Oh my little Minnie Moo!

>   MINNIE *gets* LOU*'s coat and takes it to her.*

MINNIE. Come on.

LOU. Where am I going?

MINNIE. You're walking to the Tube with Andy. You're getting some fresh air and having a talk and then you're coming back and having a cup of tea.

LOU. Okay, darling. Right.

>   LOU *gets up and* MINNIE *helps her into her coat.* MINNIE *turns the music off.*

MINNIE. Go.

LOU. What about Karl?

MINNIE. I'm looking after Karl. I'm making him a cup of tea.

LOU. I'll be back in a minute.

MINNIE. Yes. And we'll have a cup of tea. Bye, Andy.

ANDY (*no eye contact*). Bye, Minnie. See you. Well. / You know. I might.

MINNIE. Take care. Yes, see you.

ANDY. Yes.

MINNIE. Okay then. Off you go.

ANDY. Okay.

ANDY and LOU leave the flat together. MINNIE goes into the kitchen, finishes preparing the bottle and then returns with the tea.

She sits down on the sofa next to KARL. After a moment MINNIE gestures towards the bedroom.

MINNIE. I've been looking after Mary. I've been looking after Karen's baby, while she sorts herself out.

KARL. Yeah? Cool.

MINNIE. She's got a drug problem and relationship issues.

KARL. That's no good. I've had that.

MINNIE. Okay. (*Laughs.*)

Long pause.

Do you want to talk about your dad?

KARL. No you're alright.

MINNIE. Okay.

Pause.

That's fine.

Pause.

KARL. What are you, like a student?

MINNIE. I'm at university yeah.

KARL. Cool.

MINNIE. But I haven't actually been.

KARL. Okay. How does that work?

MINNIE. I went for a bit. On the first day. But I didn't, sort of fit in. With everyone else. Type of thing.

KARL. No?

MINNIE. But, y'know. I should probably go back. Give it another try.

KARL. Yeah, man.

MINNIE. I think I will.

KARL. Yeah. Go for it, girl.

> KARL *offers* MINNIE *the spliff.* MINNIE *declines.*

> *Pause.*

> D'ya get what I'm saying?

MINNIE. Yes.

KARL. What do you wanna fit in for? D'ya get me? I'm
probably not old enough to be your dad, yeah? (*Looks*
MINNIE *up and down.*) But if I was your dad, yeah? You
know? If like, say I was your dad's mate? If I was your dad's
mate, right? I would know. That your dad would want you
to. You know? Stick at it.

MINNIE. I don't really see my dad.

KARL. Shit, man. Well whatever.

MINNIE. Did you get on with your dad?

KARL. I did get on with my dad, right?

MINNIE. Well that's great –

KARL. I did get on with him, right. And I got on with my dad,
right, purely and simply, because he made it his business to
get on with me. Whatever the score was, and fuck me, I
made it hard for him, d'ya know what I'm saying? I'm a
fuck-up, basically, that's how it is. I've let stuff go. It's gone,
do you get me? And my dad. He never judged me or rejected
me or threw me out his house, right? He never said, y'know,
fuck off. Okay, little criticisms, he'd have a go, no wonder
you can't get a proper job, your trousers are halfway down
your arse. Y'know, instead of spending all your money on
drugs why don't you get yourself a belt? But not big things.
It's what he never said, you know. He never said, you
fucking owe me three and a half grand you fucking waste of
space. You are a *disappointment* to me. The decency of that
man. Respect. That's what I'm saying to you. I killed time, I
turned my back. My dad grafted. He proper sacrificed for us

kids. And I repaid him by. I fucking *stole* from that man.
Right. I stole from him. I'm sitting here now right, with you.
I don't even know you, right, and I get it. All his life my dad
followed his heart. He thought with his heart and loved with
his heart, and believed and trusted and accepted with his
heart. And forgave me. With that heart. And then. That heart
packed up on him. And they cut it out and stuck some other
bloke's heart in and sewed him up and went, off you go then,
carry on. What's that about? He fucking couldn't could he?
You can't follow someone else's heart can you? What would
be the point of that?

Silence.

MINNIE. Wow.

KARL *offers the spliff to* MINNIE. *She declines.*

KARL. Fuck, what do I know? Don't listen to me. Earlier on. I
got the call, you know from Aisling, my sister. She goes, get
yourself here, Dad's on his way out, get in the car. I said, I
can't drive, I'm off my face. She goes, get a cab, just get
here. I just sat on the step, you know. With the phone in my
hand. Nearly an hour before I called a cab. Got the call
saying he'd gone while we'd stopped at a cashpoint. Missed
him. I fucking knew I would.

Pause.

So, you know. Don't listen to me.

Pause. KARL *gets a text message. He reads it.*

MINNIE. It feels like I was sort of meant to meet you today.

KARL. Yeah? I don't believe in shit like that but if you want to
think that then that's cool.

MINNIE. I do want to think that.

KARL. Nice one. (*Stands.*) I'm gonna shoot.

MINNIE. Aren't you going to wait for Louise?

KARL. Who?

MINNIE. Lou.

KARL. I have to get to the hospital.

MINNIE. Haven't you just come from there?

KARL. No, I got there, but I didn't go in. I thought I'd swing by here. First.

MINNIE. Oh right, you better go. Aren't your family waiting for you?

KARL. Yeah, I better go.

MINNIE (*stands*). Yes. Go on.

KARL. Thanks for the cuppa.

MINNIE. Okay.

KARL. Tell Lou. Whatever. I'll call her later on or something.

MINNIE. Okay.

> KARL *stands in the middle of the room.*

KARL. Yeah. Tell her laters.

MINNIE. Quickly.

> MINNIE *moves to the door.*

KARL. Right. It's all good.

> MINNIE *opens the door and steers* KARL *out of it.* LOU *comes into the hallway.*

LOU (*off*). Where are you going?

KARL (*off*). Up the hospital.

MINNIE. He hasn't even been there yet.

LOU (*off*). Don't go yet.

KARL (*off*). Okay.

LOU (*off*). Come back in.

> LOU *and* KARL *come back in.*

MINNIE. No, Louise, he's got to go now.

LOU. He can go in a minute, you said we could have a cup of tea.

MINNIE. He's had a cup of tea,

LOU (*to* KARL). Go in a minute.

MINNIE. No, he needs to go now. His family are waiting for him.

MINNIE *steers* KARL *back out the door.*

Take care. Go straight there.

LOU. Hold on. (*Calls.*) Karl!

KARL *stands in the doorway.*

Can we just have a minute please, Minnie?

MINNIE *moves away.*

(*To* MINNIE, *a bit nasty.*) Thank you, Mum.

LOU *rolls her eyes at* KARL *behind* MINNIE*'s back.*

Are you going to be alright yeah?

KARL. Come with me.

LOU. I can't. (*Whispered.*) I can't leave her. She's, she's fragile.

KARL *looking at* LOU.

Are you going to be okay though?

KARL. Yeah. I'm good.

LOU. Are you sure yeah? (*Pause.*) Well, I really am sorry about your dad.

KARL. It's cool.

LOU. Can you leave me some gear?

Beat.

KARL. Yeah, sure.

KARL *hands* LOU *a spliff from behind his ear.*

LOU. Aah, thanks, babe. Will you call me later?

KARL. Yeah.

LOU. Text me yeah?

KARL. Yeah.

LOU. Be strong.

They kiss.

KARL *goes.* LOU *closes the door.*

LOU *comes into the room, she is sheepish.*

MINNIE. Are you alright?

LOU. Yes. Are you?

MINNIE. Yes. (*Pause.*) Karl's sweet.

LOU. Did he try and have sex with you?

MINNIE. No! His dad's just died.

LOU. I know.

Pause.

Is that baby still here?

MINNIE. Yes. She's fine, I'll take her up in the morning when Karen's back.

LOU. If she gets back.

MINNIE. She will. She wouldn't leave Mary.

LOU. I don't want her here, can't you take her somewhere else?

MINNIE. Like where?

LOU. How come you know all about her? What's going on?

MINNIE. I look after her sometimes.

LOU. For God's sake, Minnie!

MINNIE. I know. Sorry.

LOU. What were you thinking of?

MINNIE. I don't know, it just sort of started happening. I'm really sorry, Louise, I should have told you.

LOU. This is my home. I don't want her in here. I don't like it. It's a nightmare. It's totally freaking me out.

MINNIE. I'll talk to Karen tomorrow, I'll say, I won't be able to do it any more.

LOU. Yes. Tell her that.

LOU *goes into the kitchen and gets a glass of water. She drinks half and pours the rest into a plant on the windowsill.*

That's on its last legs.

MINNIE *watches* LOU.

That was a truly terrible event. Wasn't it?

MINNIE. A bit.

LOU. I mean, a monumental. A bit? Jesus!

Pause.

I have to go to bed.

LOU *moves past* MINNIE *blowing kisses.*

Kiss kiss.

MINNIE. What do you remember about my dad, Louise?

LOU. Oh my God! What? What are we talking about him for?

MINNIE. I don't know. I've been remembering some times, like at Lewes Station.

LOU. Yeah? When you were, I don't know, five, and he couldn't be bothered to meet you off that train?

MINNIE. But why was I at Lewes Station without an adult though?

LOU. Don't be insane, of course you weren't there without an adult, there was an adult. Obviously. There was that girl from the year below us, what was her name? Something. She was with you, but she'd had to go and get a connecting train, you were with a guard or, someone official was with you, it was all arranged. If Fuckface had been there it would have all gone smoothly, he fucked it up basically. He was a total waste of everybody's time.

MINNIE. I remember him crying on the front doorstep once in Sandford Street and Mum trying to close the door.

LOU. It's too late for this kind of conversation, I need to sleep. Please, Min.

MINNIE. Sorry.

LOU. It's fine, it's just. It's late.

LOU *strokes* MINNIE*'s hair.*

You have to stop seeing the good in everyone all the time, Min, it's exhausting, it's relentless, it's *unrealistic*. It's a bit, and don't take this the wrong way because I know you are terribly grown up and sensible about most things, but it's a bit immature. You know.

MINNIE. I know. Sorry.

LOU*'s phone gets a text.*

LOU. What fresh hell is this?

LOU *reads text.*

MINNIE. Please don't throw me out, Louise.

LOU. What?

MINNIE. I'm sorry about Mary, I'm sorry about talking to you all the time when you're tired. I'll change, I'll go out more, I'll be less anxious. I'm sorry, please don't make me leave.

LOU. Minnie, I'm not going to make you leave, for God's sake what are you talking about?

MINNIE. I'm sorry I messed everything up.

LOU. Stop it, is this about your dad?

MINNIE. You know, when I was little, and I used to come to London and stay with you and stuff, when Mum was, y'know, whatever. I used to pretend that you were actually my mum, that you had given birth to me and then given me to Mum as a sort of present, because you were so kind and lovely to me all the time.

LOU. Oh, Minnie. Don't.

MINNIE. And I used to wish and wish that one time you would tell me that I could come and live with you, full time, you know, in that bedroom with all your clothes and jewellery and –

LOU. Junk. Oh, Min.

MINNIE. Every time I blew out my candles I wished that.

LOU. I couldn't have had you, you know that. I would have loved to, of course I would, but I would have been hopeless. Look at me, I'm a child myself!

MINNIE. No you're not.

LOU. I am, Minnie. Look at me! Look at the mess I've made of all this, tonight. I can't do things!

MINNIE. Yes you can.

LOU. Don't think about those times, Minnie.

MINNIE. I can't help it. I'm not good at night.

LOU. Don't think about your dad. You've been fine without him haven't you? Look at you! You're at university being brilliant! What do you need him for? It's all behind you. Isn't it? Say it is, Minnie, it's exhausting you being unhappy…

MINNIE. Don't think that I'm saying you should have done more. It's just, I loved being here. You talked to me, and asked me things, you kept me safe. You didn't shut yourself away for days like Mum used to do. You saved me back then, I was so happy here with you, I was just greedy for more, that's all I'm saying.

LOU *is crying*.

Are you crying?

LOU. Of course I'm not.

Pause.

MINNIE. Don't cry.

LOU (*very quietly*). I wish I could have been your mum, Min, I would have loved to have been your mum.

MINNIE. You are like a mum.

MINNIE *and* LOU *stand in silence for a moment*.

Sorry I dredged it all up. I'm not unhappy, I promise you I'm not.

LOU. Good. You better not be.

MINNIE goes over to the sofa, she plumps up the cushions and clears KARL's mug and the ashtray. LOU watches her. MINNIE picks up the pieces of the graduation photograph. She brings them over to LOU.

Yes, sorry about that. It got ripped.

MINNIE. I can stick it.

LOU. I'll do it.

LOU takes the pieces from MINNIE.

Fuck *off*! Look at me!

MINNIE. Look at Mum!

LOU. Look at *you*! That's that bloody Doig Doig thing! I *told* you!

LOU holds the pieces together. They look at the photograph.

Sweet.

They look at the photograph.

Do I look so much older now, Min?

MINNIE. No, you look exactly the same.

LOU. You know, I see myself sometimes. It's such a shock. The shape of my body, folded up in a chair. It's like an older woman all of a sudden. The way my skin looks in direct light. The outside of me, it's racing on ahead, before I'm ready.

MINNIE. You look great.

LOU. You'll see. On *your* graduation day you'll be who you are, and you'll just carry on feeling like that. And the years roll by.

Pause.

Go to bed!

Pause.

MINNIE. Will you come to my graduation, Louise?

LOU. Of course I will! You were at mine, and I'll be at yours! That's funny isn't it?

MINNIE. Brilliant.

The baby starts to cry in MINNIE*'s room.*

LOU. Oh! / Oh God!

MINNIE. It's okay –

LOU. I can't *deal* with this now –

MINNIE. I'll do it –

LOU. I can't take any more today, I'm having a *panic* attack –

MINNIE *moves quickly to the kitchen.*

Oh God, make her stop crying for fuck's sake, Minnie! I can't stand it.

MINNIE *collects the bottle from the kitchen, tipping it up and dripping some milk on the back of her hand to test the temperature as she hurries into her bedroom.*

MINNIE. Here I am, Mary, I'm here. It's all alright now.

LOU. Urgh!

MINNIE. Night night, Louise –

LOU. Yes yes, night night, go on, give her the bottle, make her stop crying, God!

MINNIE *goes into her bedroom and closes the door.*

LOU *stands a moment and then goes into the kitchen. She opens a drawer and finds some tape, picks up the ashtray and comes into the sitting room and goes to the sofa.* LOU *very carefully tapes the pieces of the photograph together. She looks at it as she lights the spliff* KARL *gave her.*

The sound of the baby crying comes from MINNIE*'s bedroom. We hear* MINNIE*'s voice comforting the baby.*

LOU *smokes.*

Fade to black.

The End.